DEAR PILGRIM

A series of exhortations and encouragements

Diana Lovegrove

guest contributor: Elizabeth DeBarros

Published by Diana Lovegrove

Printed in the United Kingdom
First Printing, 2015
ISBN 978-0-9929204-0-1

To Peter

ACKNOWLEDGEMENTS

I have dedicated this book to my dear husband, Peter. His tender, loving care and steadfast faithfulness towards me have been the strong arm against which I have leaned and been nurtured. To be at his side as we pilgrimage together, with him leading the way, is my honour, my privilege, and my delight.

We have been blessed with the gift of a son in dear Harry. Harry, I pray that as you grow in years, you will grasp hold of the truths I have shared about in this book. May your heart's desire be to know Him, may you forsake all and count everything a loss that you may gain Christ and be found in Him.

I thank Tom Chacko, my pastor, for his insights, wisdom and love of the Lord. Our life as a family has been richly blessed by Tom and his family. He graciously agreed to review this book for me, and I am so grateful for the time he invested in this, and all that he shared. This book is all the richer for it! The very first time I ever heard Tom preach, he exhorted that we should consider the altitude of the Scriptures – and a seed was sown which has borne fruit in this book.

The Lord watered the seed for *Dear Pilgrim* through my friendship with Elizabeth DeBarros. She spoke words of faith-filled encouragement to me when I was in despair that gave me the courage to look up to Him, to wait upon Him, to reach out to Him, to ask for a touch from Him. And how He answered! Liz, I am so humbled and honoured that you would agree to allow me to include your words in this book in honour of Him, and enrich it by doing so. Thank you.

Becky Pliego, I am grateful to you for your encouragement and participation in this endeavour. May God bless you!

Hilary Hulford and Frances Piper kindly agreed to review the manuscript for grammatical errors. Thank you both, dear sisters, for your time and comments. Any remaining errors are mine alone.

My mother, Janet Reynolds, introduced me to Jesus Christ over 20 years ago. Thank you for sharing the wonderful good news with me! And to Helen, my beautiful sister, thank you for allowing me to share some of the thoughts and ideas from this book with you.

Finally, to all of my family at Gateway Christian Fellowship, I thank each and every one of you for your encouragement in the Lord, for the example you set before me, for the blessed reality that this pilgrimage to which we have been called is not one of isolation, but one to be shared in community with one another.

Diana Lovegrove
May 2015

CONTENTS

INTRODUCTION

D*ear Pilgrim* is a series of exhortations and encouragements addressed to Pilgrim, one of His called, chosen and faithful followers.

Pilgrim's journey begins in the valleys, without hope and without the Lord. But with the Lord, nothing is impossible! He is the God of the hills and the valleys. He comes down to the valley and breathes new life into Pilgrim, a lily of the valleys, a lily among thorns. As He comes, leaping across the mountains and bounding across the hills, the call is to go up. Aliyah! For the truth is that life began on a mountain in Eden, but man fell from his high place. Now, in Christ, the call is to return to the mountains, to Mount Zion.

This pilgrimage, whilst uncovering the richest of blessings and glorious treasures along the way, is costly and requires endurance. There are times when a word of encouragement and exhortation from a fellow pilgrim is gratefully received like a cup of cold water, serving to fortify and strengthen weak knees and faltering steps. My own journey has reaped the benefits of these encouragements from other faithful believers, exhorting me to look up in faith. *Dear Pilgrim* is written in this spirit.

As you read this book, I hope you will identify with Pilgrim's journey, and be strengthened and comforted in your own pilgrimage. This book is intended to encourage you to go to the Word and discover for yourself the treasures contained therein, to draw closer to the Living Word, to walk with Him on your journey in full assurance of His love for you. May you be blessed as you read, and may your eyes be lifted up to behold your God!

1.
DEAR PILGRIM, HAVE YOU ASKED HIM FOR REVELATION FROM THE PEAKS?

Dear Pilgrim, have you asked Him for revelation from the peaks? Do the mountains speak to you? Do they call out to you to come up, to come and climb, to persevere to the summit that you might be rewarded with the exhilarating view from the top?

The mountains can look daunting before you begin your ascent. You don't know how difficult the climb might be, how easy the pathway is, whether you might lose your way. You wonder if you have enough strength to make it to the top.

Pilgrim, take to heart this truth, this precious truth: the Sovereign Lord is your strength, and He makes your feet like the feet of a deer, enabling you to stand on the heights (Habakkuk 3:19). Trust Him, dear Pilgrim, to lead you up the mountains.

For it is only as we ascend the mountains that we gain His heavenly perspective. From the valleys our vision is limited. As we climb higher and higher, the panorama before our eyes expands further and further. Pilgrim, as we reflect on our journey with Him, we realise that so much of our experience of God has taken place on the mountain peaks – for it is on the mountain of the Lord that all will be provided (Genesis 22:14). He has promised that He will bring forth descendants from Jacob, and from Judah those who will possess His holy mountains, His chosen people will inherit them, and there His servants will live (Isaiah 65:9). We are called to live on the mountains, dear Pilgrim! As we journey with Him, we have many valleys to cross, but we are always heading upwards to Zion.

Who may ascend the mountain of the Lord? The one who has clean hands and a pure heart (Psalm 24:3-4). There is only One who possesses these – but now that we are found in Him, He has given us clean hands and a pure heart, Pilgrim! So come, let us ascend the mountain of the Lord!

It was on a mountain in Eden that Adam was placed – for the rivers flowed down from this garden (Genesis 2:10). Life began for man on the mountains. Glory! Yet man fell from this place of honour down to the valleys below, as he succumbed to the temptation of sin, and fell short of the glory of God.

It was to the mountains that He told us to flee for our lives that we might find refuge, not to look back, not to stop anywhere on the plain, or we would be swept away in the wrath to come (Genesis 19:17).

It was on Mount Sinai that our Holy God revealed His

law to Moses. It was from another mountain that Jesus preached a sermon expounding the full extent of that Holy Law. As we meditated on all that was revealed, we were broken before our Holy God.

It was on a high mountain that His disciples bowed before the revelation of the Glory of Jesus as He was transfigured before them.

David wept as he went up the Mount of Olives (2 Samuel 15:30). It was at this very same place that the Son of David was overwhelmed with sorrow, praying so earnestly that His sweat was like drops of blood falling to the ground, as He contemplated the suffering to come on account of our sin (Luke 22:39-44).

It was from a hill called Golgotha that Jesus Himself paid the penalty for our sins against a Holy God through His atoning death, which bought our redemption, gave us forgiveness of sins, and brought about reconciliation with our Heavenly Father.

It is to the mountains of Israel that He has brought His lost sheep to be pastured, and our grazing land is on the mountain heights of Israel, where we lie down and feed in a rich pasture (Ezekiel 34:13-14).

It was from the Mount of Olives that the Risen Jesus ascended to Heaven. Now at the right hand of the Father, He has become our High Priest and Mediator.

It will be to the Mount of Olives that Jesus will return again in glory (Zechariah 14:4), to bring salvation to His Bride.

God reveals Himself from the mountains. The apostle John recounts: "One of the seven angels who had the seven bowls full of the seven last plagues came and said to me, 'Come, I will show you the bride, the wife of the Lamb'. And he carried me away in the Spirit to a mountain great and high, and showed me the Holy City, Jerusalem, coming down out of heaven from God" (Revelation 21:9-10).

In these days in which we are living, Pilgrim, I believe we would do well to cry out to God to take us to the tops of the mountains, that He may grant us to see with a clearer vision.

2.
DEAR PILGRIM, HAVE YOU HEARD CREATION GROANING?

Dear Pilgrim, have you heard creation groaning? You have heard the cries of a woman labouring in childbirth – did you realise that creation groans and labours with birth pangs? For the beautiful creation we see today, which clearly reveals the invisible attributes of our faithful Creator, bears the scars and wounds of a very dark day.

O Pilgrim, behold the Garden. The beautiful, glorious, magnificent Garden of Eden. This Garden high up on a mountain. This Garden which was planted by the Gardener Himself, who carefully chose each plant, shrub, and flower to provide a feast for the eyes of colour, an aromatic bouquet of perfection, textures beyond compare. The rivers of delight joyfully flowed through the Garden, causing all that was planted to flourish. O, clap your hands in joy and give thanks to the Creator of the heavens, who stretches them out, who spreads out the earth with all that springs from it, who gives breath to its people, and life to those who walk in it, give thanks to Him and lift up your voice with the sound of singing!

Pilgrim, there were many animals in the Garden. So many different species, all made according to their kind. The lion ate straw like the ox, whilst the wolf and the lamb fed together (Isaiah 65:25), for the Lord God gave the animals every green plant to eat (Genesis 1:30). And the birds, innumerable varieties, sang so many different songs in praise to their Creator, what a symphony of praise! O Pilgrim, can we do anything other than shout out our own praises to our great God as we consider this beautiful world? Blessed be Your glorious Name, and may it be exalted above all blessing and praise! You alone are the Lord! You made the heavens, even the highest heavens, and all their starry host, the earth and all that is on it, the seas and all that is in them. You give life to everything, and the multitudes of heaven worship You (Nehemiah 9:6).

Pilgrim, behold Adam and Eve in the Garden. Created in the very image of God, in His likeness, to rule over the fish of the sea, the birds in the sky and over every living creature that moves on the ground. Created to enjoy fellowship with the Triune God, to work and take care of His Garden.

O Pilgrim – with fear and trembling let us recall the events which took place thereafter. A serpent! A shadow of darkness. The crunch as teeth took a bite from the forbidden fruit. The rustle of leaves being pulled from trees in haste. The sound of the Lord God walking in the garden in the cool of the day. His voice calling, "Where are you?" Human voices responding in shame. His voice speaking again...such grief in His voice. Yet within the grief, a promise was made, a promise that brought joy through the sorrow (Genesis 3:15).

For even as dark shadows fell across the face of the earth, as Adam and Eve left the Garden, they were clothed in hope. They were clothed, not in fig leaves of their own choosing, their own feeble attempt to cover themselves, but in clothing provided by their Redeemer, made by His very own hands. They were clothed in the skin of the very first animal sacrifice – a horrific scarring of creation. As that sacrifice was made, the unfamiliar stench of death filled the Garden. It clung to Adam and Eve as they walked out of the Garden. Yet even so, these skins were a symbol of hope, for not only was their shame covered over, but this animal sacrifice pointed to the One to come in fulfilment of the Promise – the Lamb of God who takes away the sin of the world!

And so it was that sin entered the world through one man, and death through sin (Romans 5:12). The entrance of sin into the world was such a heinous act that creation itself has been marred and cursed as a result. Death came to creation. Death came to a world where all that had been known was life. And now creation bears the scars of our sin. As thorns and thistles grow out of the ground, animal turns upon animal, and the earth cries out at the blood that has been spilt. The agonized cry of creation.

But Pilgrim, this is not the final cry of creation! No! For creation has been subjected to frustration, not by its

9

own choice, but by the One who subjected it in hope (Romans 8:20). It has been cursed in hope – for the Promise that was uttered in the Garden, the Promise that brought joy in the midst of sorrow, this Promise is 'Yes' in Christ! The first Adam, through his disobedience, brought death. The last Adam, through His obedience, died to sin once for all, that we might be clothed in His righteousness, and He will destroy the last enemy – death. Creation will be liberated from its bondage to decay and will be brought into the freedom and glory of the children of God.

And the song we will hear on that day? Why, the trees of the field shall clap their hands! The fields will be jubilant, and everything in them, the trees of the forest will sing for joy! All of creation will rejoice before the Lord when He comes to judge the earth in faithfulness (Psalm 96:12-13)! And once again, the wolf will live with the lamb and they will feed together.

3.
DEAR PILGRIM, HAS HE BREATHED UPON YOU?

Dear Pilgrim, has He breathed upon you? Has the living God breathed life into you?

For so long, dear Pilgrim, you chased after the wind. When you surveyed all your hands had done, all you had toiled to achieve, you saw that everything was meaningless, a chasing after the wind, that nothing was gained under the sun (Ecclesiastes 2:11). You saw that everyone, yourself included, is senseless and without knowledge, shamed by the idols they trust in, for those images are false – for they have no breath in them (Jeremiah 10:14).

But God, the God who gives breath to all living things, came and He called your name. The One in whose hand is the life of every creature and the breath of all mankind (Job 12:10) came near. The One who made the heavens by His word and their starry host by the breath of His mouth (Psalm 33:6) came close to you.

He came so close that He breathed into your nostrils –
He gave you the kiss of life.

He breathed, and His breath came from the four winds
(Ezekiel 37:9).

He breathed, and the east wind came! The east wind
came in judgement to scorch, to wither and shrivel up the
fruit of the world from you (Ezekiel 19:12). For this fruit
has no place in Him, this fruit that you bore for death
(Romans 7:5). It was consumed by the east wind of
judgement.

He breathed, and the north wind came! The north
wind came in power and brought an unexpected storm
upon you (Proverbs 25:23). You saw clearly for the first
time your meaningless chasing after the wind. O Pilgrim,
how you cried out to Him as you stood there, stripped
and naked before Him, as the storm blew away all the fig
leaves that you had attempted to clothe yourself in, your
own righteousness of filthy rags ripped away by the
powerful north wind.

He breathed, and the west wind came! The west wind
carried your sins and iniquities far away (Exodus 10:19).
The west wind came and hurled your iniquities into the
depths of the sea. As far as the east is from the west, so far
has He removed our transgressions from us (Psalm
103:12).

He breathed, and the south wind came! The gentle
south wind (Acts 27:13) brought a hush and calmness
upon you (Job 37:17) as He clothed your nakedness with
His own righteousness. For the first time you rested in
Him. A wondrous peace came into your heart as

realisation dawned on you that you had been reconciled to Him. He gave you the kiss of life – and righteousness and peace kissed each other deep within your heart (Psalm 85:10), the heart that He had now won for Himself.

So His breath came from the four winds, and brought life (Ezekiel 37:9). The One who rebuked the wind (Mark 4:39-41) and terrified His disciples when they saw how the wind obeyed Him came, and He breathed upon you and said, "Receive the Holy Spirit" (John 20:22). And for the first time you were able to exclaim, "The Spirit of God has made me, the breath of the Almighty gives me life!" (Job 33:4). And you began to see that it is the spirit in a person, the breath of the Almighty, that gives them understanding (Job 32:8), for understanding comes from the mouth of the Lord (Proverbs 2:6).

O Pilgrim, you now see how meaningless it is to trust in idols. For when those who trust in them cry out for help, the wind will carry the idols off, a mere breath will blow them away (Isaiah 57:13). There is no breath in the mouth of the idols (Psalm 135:17). But His breath, the breath of the living God, is like a rushing torrent, rising up to the neck (Isaiah 30:28). The breath of God produces ice, and the broad waters become frozen (Job 37:10). The valleys of the sea are exposed and the foundations of the earth are laid bare at His rebuke, at the blast of breath from His nostrils (2 Samuel 22:16). With righteousness He will come and He will strike the earth with the rod of His mouth; with the breath of His lips He will slay the wicked (Isaiah 11:4). The Lord Jesus

13

will overthrow the lawless one with the breath of His mouth and destroy him by the splendour of His coming (2 Thessalonians 2:8). Who is like our God?

O Pilgrim, as we tremble, watching and waiting for His return, may we draw close to Him. May we lean against His breast, just as the beloved disciple did, and who was later chosen to receive a great revelation from Him. For the One who creates the wind is the One who reveals His thoughts to mankind (Amos 4:13). May the God-breathed words of Scripture be our meditation and our food, as He unfolds His words to give us understanding. May the fragrance of our breath be to God the pleasing aroma of Christ among those who are being saved and those who are perishing. And may He receive praise from everything that has breath!

4.
DEAR PILGRIM, ARE YOU HEEDING THE CALL TO FLEE FOR YOUR LIFE?

Dear Pilgrim, are you heeding the call to flee for your life? Are you refusing to neither look back, nor stop anywhere on the plain? Are you fleeing to the mountains so that you will not be swept away (Genesis 19:17)?

Pilgrim, the time is short, for this is the last hour (1 John 2:18). The warning is to be taken to heart – for how shall we escape if we ignore such a great salvation? "Now is the day of salvation" (2 Corinthians 6:2). Are we heeding the call to flee for our lives?

For the wrath of God is coming. The day of God's wrath is coming, when His righteous judgment will be revealed, for the outcry against the people is so great, their sin is so grievous. On that day, people will flee to caves in the rocks and to holes in the ground from the fearful presence of the Lord and the splendour of His majesty, when He rises to shake the earth (Isaiah 2:19).

The heavens will tremble, the earth will shake from its place at the wrath of the Lord Almighty, in the day of His burning anger. But for those who have ears to hear, the gospel call rings out loud and clear: "Flee for your lives!"

Pilgrim, flee! Flee from Babylon! Run for your life! Do not be destroyed because of her sins. Flee from sexual immorality (1 Corinthians 6:18)! Flee from idolatry (1 Corinthians 10:14)! Flee from the love of money (1 Timothy 6:10)! Flee the evil desires of youth (2 Timothy 2:22)!

Pilgrim, do not look back. Do not stop anywhere on the plain. For "no-one who puts a hand to the plough and looks back is fit for service in the kingdom of God" (Luke 9:62). Follow the example of Rebekah, called to leave her home to become the wife of Isaac. She chose to leave her family immediately rather than stay a further ten days at home (Genesis 24:58). She recognised the urgency of the call.

O Pilgrim, remember Lot's wife. "Lot's wife looked back, and she became a pillar of salt" (Genesis 19:26). Let us not look back with any yearning for our old way of life. We used to follow the ways of this world, gratifying the cravings of the flesh, following its desires and thoughts. But in Christ we heard the gospel call, which rings out loud and clear: "Flee for your lives!" Having been alienated from God because of our evil behaviour, now we have been reconciled to Him through Christ and we are now foreigners and strangers here on earth. We are now foreigners even to our own family, a stranger to our own mother's children. But Pilgrim, let us not look back.

Flee, Pilgrim! Flee to the City of Refuge. Just as the six cities of refuge provided protection for a fugitive from the wrath of those seeking vengeance in the land of Israel, so Christ is our Refuge to save us from the wrath of God to come. Flee to Him, Pilgrim. Blessed are all who take refuge in the Son, who kiss the Son (Psalm 2:12). O, kiss the Son, Pilgrim, bow at His feet and worship Him. Take refuge in the shadow of His wings. For no-one who takes refuge in Him will be condemned. No one! They will be glad, for He has stored up good things in abundance for those who fear Him. Not only so, but He will bestow these good things on those who take refuge in Him in the sight of all.

So run, Pilgrim, run to His Name! For the Name of the Lord is a fortified tower; the righteous run to it and are safe (Proverbs 18:10). His Name protected His disciples and kept them safe when He walked this earth, and His Name continues to protect His own. Bearing His Name, desiring to honour Him in everything, run with perseverance the race marked out for you. Run in the path of His commands, Pilgrim, keep running, and you will find yourself ascending, leaving behind the valley, leaving behind the plains.

It is to the mountains that we are fleeing. The mountains! For His promise stands firm and solid: "Whoever takes refuge in Me will inherit the land and possess My holy mountain" (Isaiah 57:13). As we flee to Christ we will possess His holy mountain. We will dwell on the heights and our refuge will be the mountain fortress (Isaiah 33:16). For it is on Mount Zion that His people

17

will find refuge. Mount Zion, the city of the living God. Those He has redeemed will enter Zion with singing; and as they do so, it will be sorrow and sighing which will flee away (Isaiah 35:10). There is a day coming when the Lord will create over all of Mount Zion and over those who assemble there a cloud of smoke by day and a glow of flaming fire by night; over everything the glory will be a canopy. The glory of God! It will be a shelter and shade from the heat of the day, and a refuge and hiding-place from the storm and rain (Isaiah 4:5-6).

O Pilgrim, flee to Him, run to Him, and you will be richly blessed!

5.
DEAR PILGRIM, HAVE YOU BEEN BROKEN BY HIS HOLY LAW?

Dear Pilgrim, have you been broken by His Holy law? Have you trembled and been shaken at the revelation of His holiness? Have you been utterly undone as He has revealed His law to you?

Behold - Mount Sinai! A mountain like no other. For it was on this mountain that He chose to reveal His holiness to His people. It was on this mountain that He came down and spoke to His people from heaven.

As the Israelites gathered at this mountain having been brought out of captivity from Egypt, the Lord said to Moses: "I am going to come to you in a dense cloud, so that the people will hear Me speaking with you and will always put their trust in you" (Exodus 19:9). The Lord was going to come down on Mount Sinai in the presence of all the people.

He descended upon Mount Sinai in fire – the peak was covered in smoke, there was thunder, lightning, and the sound of trumpets! The whole mountain trembled violently.

Only Moses was given permission by the Lord to ascend this mountain. Mount Sinai was not to be climbed by the people. O Pilgrim, is it any wonder that the people trembled with fear and stayed at a distance, imploring Moses, "Speak to us yourself and we will listen. But do not have God speak to us or we will die" (Exodus 20:19).

Having spoken with the Lord, Moses came back down the mountain and told the people all of the Lord's words and His holy laws. The people responded with one voice, "Everything the Lord has said we will do" (Exodus 24:3). The law, followed in faith, obedience and humility, would reveal to His people their need of a Saviour and of a perfect sacrifice for all their sins.

However, those who chose instead to establish their own righteousness through works of the law pursued a path that led to death. For the truth is that it is through the law that we become conscious of sin. This holy law, this holy, righteous and good commandment, reveals the righteous requirements of our holy, holy, holy God. But there is no one righteous, not even one (Romans 3:10). We are unable to keep His law because of the fallen nature we inherited from Adam. This holy law brings wrath, for all have sinned and fall short of the glory of God (Romans 3:23). As we listen to the law and the righteous requirements of our Holy God, we dare not even look up to heaven, all we can do is beat our breasts and cry out to the Lord, "God, have mercy on me, a sinner!"

But what the law was powerless to do because it was weakened by the flesh, God did by sending His own Son in the likeness of sinful flesh on account of sin (Romans 8:3). O Pilgrim, let us behold another mountain, which the One who came to have mercy on sinners climbed.

Crowds of people came to this mountain, as at Mount Sinai. But this time, His disciples were able to climb the mountain to be with Him! There was no smoke on this mountain, no thunder, no lightning, no trumpets – but there was the Son of God! Where the people could not touch Mount Sinai, here they could touch the Son of God!

Listen as He poured out blessings upon His disciples by saying, "Blessed are the poor in spirit, for theirs is the kingdom of heaven" (Matthew 5:3). Blessings for those who see how far short they have fallen of the righteous requirements of the law! Then listen to His words which followed: "Do not think that I have come to abolish the Law or the Prophets; I have not come to abolish them but to fulfil them" (Matthew 5:17). For He is the Righteous One, He is holy, blameless, pure, set apart from sinners (Hebrews 7:26), for He committed no sin. He fulfilled the law!

Listen as the One who fulfilled the law said to His disciples, "Be perfect, therefore, as your heavenly Father is perfect" (Matthew 5:48).

Pilgrim – do these words not cut you to the heart? Do these words not bring revelation of how far short we have fallen of the glory of God? Do these words not strip us of all our self-righteousness, of any attempt to hold up our own works for justification before Him?

21

O Pilgrim, may these words do their work in us. May these words, sharper than any double-edged sword, cut right to our hearts. May the Great Physician strip us of self, empty us of self. For no-one will be declared righteous in God's sight by works of the law.

And then, dear Pilgrim, oh, what sweet truth is this... let us cry out to Him in repentance from our works which are as filthy rags, let us cry out to the Righteous One who fulfilled the holy law, and He will send His Spirit, the Spirit who sets us free from the law of sin and death! Let us cry out to Him, and He will send the Spirit of power, the Spirit of Him who raised Jesus from the dead! The Spirit who gives life! Let us cry out in faith, believing all we have heard, and His righteousness will be ours! Justification will be ours!

And as we take to heart this truth, we will find that we will die to the law through the body of Christ that we might live for God. We will be crucified with Christ, and we will no longer live but Christ will live in us. As we work out our salvation with fear and trembling, He will work in us to will and to act in order to fulfil His good purpose (Philippians 2:13).

So let us live by the Spirit, not gratifying the desires of the flesh, but bearing fruit, beautiful fruit, for God! O Pilgrim, join with me in looking out at the view from atop this mountain, and let us rejoice in the truth that we have found up here!

6.
DEAR PILGRIM, HAS HE STRIPPED YOU OF YOUR PRIDE?

Dear Pilgrim, has He stripped you of your pride? Has He unclasped the necklace of pride that used to grace your neck? Has He brought you low that He might revive your spirit?

Pilgrim, rejoice that He has dealt so severely with you, for the Lord disciplines those He loves. He chastens everyone He accepts as a son (Hebrews 12:5-6). For God disciplines us for our good, in order that we might share in His holiness (Hebrews 12:10).

Man has always been seeking to make a name for himself. One of man's earliest attempts to exalt himself was by making a tower that reached to the heavens, the Tower of Babel. In rebellion against God, man trusted in his own strength and began to build. But unless the Lord builds the house, the builders labour in vain. So the Lord God came down, the High and Lofty One came down from His high and holy place to see the city and the tower that man was building. The potter came down to see the deeds of the clay. And He performed mighty deeds with His arm; He scattered those who are proud in their inmost thoughts (Luke 1:51). He scattered them over the face of the earth.

Yet man in his stubbornness felt no pain; when the Lord crushed him, he refused correction. He made his face harder than stone and refused to repent (Jeremiah 5:3). For even though he was wearied by all his ways, he would not say, 'It is hopeless'. He found renewal of his strength, so he did not faint (Isaiah 57:10). Man strengthened himself. Oh, what folly! For in his pride the wicked man does not seek God; in all his thoughts there is no room for his Creator (Psalm 10:4).

Pride – the source and root of all sin. O Pilgrim, how wicked is the proud heart that seeks to be independent of God and trusts in itself for wisdom. Was this not the temptation to which Adam and Eve succumbed in the Garden? They listened to the lie that if they ate of the fruit of the tree of the knowledge of good and evil, they could be like God, knowing good and evil for themselves. They chose the way of pride, rather than walking in submission with their God. They chose to listen to the father of lies, rather than the Father of the Heavenly Lights, who had given them every good and perfect gift from above.

O Pilgrim, listen to the heart of God as He sings this lament to the father of lies: "You were the seal of perfection, full of wisdom and perfect in beauty. You were in Eden, the garden of God...you were anointed as a guardian cherub, for so I ordained you. You were on the holy mount of God...You were blameless in your ways from the day you were created till wickedness was found in you. So I drove you in disgrace from the mount of God...Your heart became proud on account of your beauty, and you corrupted your wisdom because of your splendour. So I threw you to the earth" (Ezekiel 28:12-17).

He was on the holy mount of God, Pilgrim, he was perfect in beauty. But his heart became proud. It was not enough to be in this wonderful position of privilege and honour. He wanted more. The holy mount of God did not meet his ambitions. For it was he who said in his heart, "I will ascend to the heavens; I will raise my throne above the stars of God; I will sit enthroned on the mount of assembly, on the utmost heights of Mount Zaphon" (Isaiah 14:13).

Mount Zaphon, the sacred mountain of the Canaanites. Mount Zaphon, majestic in height. But a mountain of his own choosing. Not the chosen mountain. A king of his own choosing. Not the chosen King. For it is not Mount Zaphon, but Mount Zion, which is His dwelling-place. "Beautiful in its loftiness, the joy of the whole earth, like the heights of Zaphon is Mount Zion, the city of the Great King" (Psalm 48:2). And it is not the guardian cherub who will be king. For He says, "I have installed My King on Zion, My holy mountain" (Psalm 2:6).

"Rejoice greatly, Daughter Zion! Shout, Daughter Jerusalem! See, your king comes to you, righteous and victorious, lowly and riding on a donkey, on a colt, the foal of a donkey" (Zechariah 9:9).

O Pilgrim, rejoice that He has come to you, rejoice that He has stripped you of your pride. For you no longer belong to the devil, you have been brought into the Kingdom of the Son He loves. Have the same mindset as Christ, who humbled Himself by becoming obedient to death – even death on a cross. For thus says the High and Lofty One who inhabits eternity, whose Name is Holy: "I live in a high and holy place, but also with him who is contrite and lowly in spirit, to revive the spirit of the lowly and to revive the heart of the contrite" (Isaiah 57:15).

7.
DEAR PILGRIM, HAVE YOU BEHELD THE LAMB OF GOD?

Dear Pilgrim, have you beheld the Lamb of God? The Lamb of God, who takes away the sin of the world? Have you looked upon the Lamb who was slain?

O Pilgrim, let us remember Golgotha, the hill outside Jerusalem. Golgotha, the place of the skull. Golgotha, the place where He was lifted up from the earth. Surely this is holy ground!

Pilgrim, does the remembrance of Golgotha not cause us to tremble? For here He took up our pain, and bore our suffering. He was pierced for our transgressions, and crushed for our iniquities. The Lord laid on Him the iniquity of us all. O Pilgrim, He bore our sins in His body on the cross. He bore my sin. He bore your sin.

When Abraham declared to Isaac, "God Himself will provide the lamb for the burnt offering, my son" (Gen 22:8), could he have known how these words would be fulfilled? On the mountain of the Lord it will be provided, and here, on the mountain of the Lord, the Lamb, the Lamb of God who takes away the sin of the world, was provided.

Just as the Passover Lamb was a lamb without defect, so Jesus Christ was a lamb without blemish or defect (1 Peter 1:19). Pilate declared after examining the Lamb, "I find no basis for a charge against Him" (John 19:6). Behold, the Lamb of God, who takes away the sin of the world!

Jesus Christ, our Passover Lamb, was led like a lamb to the slaughter, and as a sheep before its shearers is silent, so He did not open His mouth (Isaiah 53:7). For Jesus made no reply, not to a single charge that was brought against Him (Matthew 27:14). Behold, the Lamb of God, who takes away the sin of the world!

He was like one from whom people hid their faces, for He was despised and held in low esteem. O Pilgrim, let us not hide our faces from Him! Let us fix our eyes upon our Saviour, who spilt His blood for you and for me, who poured out His blood for many for the forgiveness of sins. Behold, the Lamb of God, who takes away the sin of the world!

Behold the Bread of Affliction upon the cross (Deuteronomy 16:3). The bread of affliction, bread made without yeast, was eaten, along with the Passover Lamb, by the Israelites in remembrance of the night they fled Egypt. The Bread of Life, the living bread that came down from heaven, became the Bread of Affliction that we might eat of His flesh which He gave for the life of the world.

The Bread of Affliction cried out, "I am thirsty", in order to fulfil the Scriptures. A jar of wine vinegar was there, so they soaked a sponge in it, put the sponge on a stalk of the hyssop plant, and lifted it to Jesus' lips. As they did so, they lay before us the meal that Ruth's kinsman-redeemer offered to her, when he gave her a meal of bread dipped in wine vinegar (Ruth 2:14).

Pilgrim, recall the words Boaz speaks to Ruth as she shares this meal: "I've been told...how you left your father and mother and your homeland and came to live with a people you did not know before. May the Lord repay you for what you have done. May you be richly rewarded by the Lord, the God of Israel, under whose wings you have come to take refuge" (Ruth 2:11-12).

O Pilgrim, how can it be that He would speak in this manner to us? How can we have found such favour in His eyes? How can it be that He would give such comfort to us, and speak so kindly to us, when it is our sin which has caused His suffering, when it is because of our own sin that He hangs on this cross?

Yet He does indeed speak these words to you who have left everything to come and kneel at the foot of His cross, you who have fled the city where you dwelt to find refuge in the mountains. You will be richly rewarded by the Lord, the God of Israel, under whose wings you have come to take refuge. For it is in His cross that you have come to take refuge, it is in His cross where you shelter in the shadow of His wings, it is in His cross that you are covered by His blood – His blood in which a rich reward is to be found.

For His blood of the new covenant was poured out for many, for the forgiveness of sins. We, who were in slavery to sin, have been redeemed through His blood. We, who were far away, have been brought near by His blood. He has cleansed our consciences from acts that lead to death through His blood. We have been reconciled with our Father in heaven through His blood. We have peace with God through His blood. He makes us holy through His blood. We have been purified from sin through His blood. He has freed us from our sins through His blood. We will overcome by the blood of the Lamb.

O Pilgrim, what precious blood this is! What riches there are in His blood! O Pilgrim, at one and the same time are our hearts not filled with grief that He had to pour out His blood, yet filled with rejoicing at what has been accomplished? What can we do but bow down and worship? Let us join with the angels in singing, "Worthy is the Lamb, who was slain, to receive power and wealth and wisdom and strength and honour and glory and praise!"

8.
DEAR PILGRIM, ARE YOU STRUGGLING WITH CONDEMNATION?

Dear Pilgrim, are you struggling with condemnation? Are voices whispering to you that you are no good, leaving you in despair? Are you feeling crushed in your spirit?

O Pilgrim, how I understand! But despair never has the final word for the Christian. Let us consider the Garden to which our Lord was taken after the crucifixion. Recall the tomb hewn from the rock, the tomb where the body of Jesus was laid, in apparent defeat. But on Resurrection Day, the stone was removed from the entrance. The strips of linen were lying there, and the burial cloth that had been around His head was folded up by itself, separate from the linen. The tomb was empty. It was empty, dear Pilgrim! He was not there – for He had risen! For God exerted His mighty strength in Christ and raised Him from the dead (Ephesians 1:19). God raised this Jesus to life!

This Garden was not far from where the Lamb of God died upon the cross for the forgiveness of our sins, paying the wages of death for our sin. But how easily we forget to consider the empty tomb, to marvel at the victory that has been won. The enemy will do all he can to distract us from spending time reflecting on the empty tomb and all that it means – for this is the place of our Lord's great victory!

For the truth of this glorious gospel message into which we have been brought by the blood of the Lamb does not end with the blessed news that our sins and iniquities have been forgiven. O Pilgrim, behold the revelation of the empty tomb which speaks of new life! The revelation of the empty tomb which speaks of the power of the Spirit! The revelation of the empty tomb which speaks of the victory that He has won!

For if we have been baptised into Christ, we have been baptised into His death. Our old self was crucified with Him. Not only were we baptised into the death of Christ – we were buried with Him. Our old self is crucified, dead and buried. It no longer has power over us. We no longer identify with it. It is defeated! We were buried with Him through baptism into death in order that, just as Christ was raised from the dead through the glory of the Father, we too may live a new life. A new life, Pilgrim! No longer a life of slavery to sin, a life of captivity, a life without hope, a life that was no life for it led to death. No matter how many times the enemy tries to whisper to you that you have no hope, that you cannot escape the clutches of sin, that you are guilty, the truth is that now that we have died we have been set free from sin (Romans 6:7)! Yes, Pilgrim, we do daily still wrestle with sin, we daily have to fight against sin, but it is no longer our master. For we have been set free from the power of sin. Set free from the guilt of sin. Set free from the penalty of sin. Set free from the slavery of sin. It was for freedom that Christ has set us free. O Pilgrim, rejoice that your chains are gone. Gone! No longer a slave – a son! A child of God!

Pilgrim, it must have been quiet in that Garden, quiet on those days when Jesus lay there in the tomb. Maybe some thought it was the quiet despair of defeat. It may have looked like defeat, as the Creator bowed His head and breathed His last. It may have looked like defeat, as His lifeless body lay in the tomb for three days. It may have looked like defeat, as all was silent. But His final words, "It is finished!" continued to ring with the glorious sounds of triumph and victory as they resounded through the heavens, as they made the powers and authorities shudder in fear. And then, in the fullness of time, the Voice of the Lord spoke, and shook the earth. The Voice of the Lord thundered. There was a violent earthquake, the Son of God was raised to life – for it was impossible for death to keep its hold on Him. The power of the Spirit raised Him to life. Victory! But not His victory alone. For thanks be to God! He gives us the victory through our Lord Jesus Christ (1 Corinthians 15:57). We have been raised up and seated with Christ in the heavenly realms. We are more than conquerors through Him who loved us.

Pilgrim, because of the empty tomb and the victory He

has won, the victory He gives to us, this means we have peace with God! What were the very first words He uttered to His disciples after He arose? "Peace be with you!" (John 20:19). Who is the one who condemns? Not God! For Christ Jesus who died – more than that, who was raised to life – is at the right hand of God, interceding for us (Romans 8:34). Interceding, Pilgrim, not condemning. There is now no condemnation for those who are in Christ Jesus, because through Christ Jesus the law of the Spirit, who gives life, has set you free from the law of sin and death (Romans 8:1). You are free, free from the law of sin and death, free to put to death the misdeeds of the body, free to be led by the Spirit of God, free to walk in righteousness, free to overcome the world!

Pilgrim, never forget the empty tomb. The enemy will do all he can to keep you from taking in all that it means, for it is the empty tomb that reveals that he is defeated. Resist him, and he will flee! And may the truth of the empty tomb be engraved on your heart.

9.
DEAR PILGRIM, ARE YOU HUNGRY?

Dear Pilgrim, are you hungry? Have you had your fill from eating loaves? Or rather than seeking for food that spoils, are you searching for food that endures to eternal life?

The Lord our God is the perfect host. There is a feast forever on offer from the abundance of His house (Psalm 36:8)! He planted a Garden for man, overflowing and teeming with good food from the trees, watered as they were by the rivers of the Spirit, the rivers of delight. How it was His desire that we should eat and be satisfied, that we would delight in the overflowing abundance of all He freely offered.

Yet man turned his back on the feast of faith - and ever since the ground has been subject to a curse, such that only through painful toil can man now eat food from it. Thorns and thistles now point to the glory from which man has fallen. All the toil of man is for his mouth, yet his appetite is not satisfied (Ecclesiastes 6:7). With a heart set on earthly things, even the riches of the promised inheritance from the Lord are sold for a pot of stew. Yet still man's appetite is not satisfied.

For food that spoils can never satisfy. But there is another food – and this food endures for eternal life. It was in the desert as men gave in to their cravings that this was revealed, as they tested the living God by asking, "Can God really spread a table in the wilderness?" (Psalm 78:19). Is the arm of the Lord too short? Can He not instruct His ravens to bring bread and meat to His servants? So the merciful Father opened the doors of the heavens, He rained down manna from heaven, and man ate the bread of angels.

Dear Pilgrim, are you hungry? There is One who has food to eat that we know nothing about (John 4:32). His food is to do the will of His Father and to finish His work (John 4:34). As the Bread of Affliction (Deuteronomy 16:3) hung upon the cross, He purchased salvation for you and for me by giving His flesh for the life of the world (John 6:51). As the Living Bread was raised to life, He gives us eternal life and promises to raise us up at the last day (John 6:54).

Dear Pilgrim, are you feeding on Him? For man shall not live on bread alone, but on every word that proceeds from the mouth of God. Today, if you hear His voice, do not harden your heart (Hebrews 4:7). Are you feeding on Him? When His Word comes, will you eat it? For His Word is our joy and our heart's delight (Jeremiah 15:16). His Word is as sweet as honey. Will you open your mouth and eat what He gives you (Ezekiel 2:8)? For He will fill the hungry with good things, but the rich He will send away empty (Luke 1:53).

Dear Pilgrim, do you see the table He has prepared for you? This table is in the presence of your enemies (Psalm 23:5) – but precious Pilgrim, there is no need to fear. Be strong! For the Bread of the Presence is always at His table (Exodus 25:30). Oh, let Him lead you to the banquet hall (Song of Songs 2:4)! You may well protest, "What is Your servant, that You should notice a dead dog like me?" (2 Samuel 9:8). But remember, even the dogs eat the crumbs that fall from their master's table (Matthew 15:27). O Pilgrim, is it possible to grasp the full glory of the inheritance into which He has brought us – that we are to eat at the King's table like one of the King's sons (2 Samuel 9:11)? Is it possible? Can this be true? O Pilgrim, yes, this is true! Sit no longer in the shadows, grateful simply to be in His company, longing for a glance to come your way from His table, yet not daring to hope that He might notice you. Rather, it is His desire that you take your seat at His table, to eat and drink with Him! To look at Him full in the face, to speak to Him, and delight in the sound of His voice speaking to you.

Precious Pilgrim, you have been watching for Him, waiting for Him, you have been wise and have taken oil in your lamp to keep it burning. Take to heart this truth - He will dress Himself to serve, He will make you recline at His table, He will come to wait on you (Luke 12:37)! The One before whom every knee will bow and every tongue confess that He is Lord, to the glory of the Father....He will come to wait on you! This is our God! O Pilgrim...when He reveals these truths in His Word.....the abundance, the love He lavishes on us....sometimes it is almost too much to take in. The riches of His glorious inheritance...let us fall to our knees in worship. Who is like our God (Psalm 113:5-8)?

O Pilgrim, come, come to Mount Zion! This is where the feast is laid out before us! Come, come and feast in the abundance of His house! Oh come, come to His table! And let us go to the street corners and invite anyone we can find, who has ears to listen, to come and feast with us at this banquet!

On this mountain the Lord Almighty will prepare
a feast of rich food for all peoples,
a banquet of aged wine –
the best of meats and the finest of wines.
(Isa 25:6)

10.
DEAR PILGRIM, DOES CHRIST DWELL IN YOUR HEART THROUGH FAITH?

Dear Pilgrim, does Christ dwell in your heart through faith? Are you asking Him to strengthen you out of His glorious riches with power through His Spirit in your inner being, that Christ may dwell in your heart through faith (Ephesians 3:17)? I ask that He will do this for you and for me, Pilgrim friend, for we need Him there as we walk this pilgrim path!

You may be thinking to yourself, how can Christ dwell in my heart, when the heart of man is deceitful above all things, and desperately wicked (Jeremiah 17:9)? How can Christ dwell in my heart, when out of the heart come evil thoughts – murder, adultery, sexual immorality, theft, false testimony, slander (Matthew 15:19)? Maybe you are thinking, as I did for so many years, that you will not be blessed by seeing God for your heart is not pure (Matthew 5:8).

If so, the cry of your heart is the cry of the Pilgrim

throughout the ages: "Create in me a pure heart, O God, and renew a steadfast spirit within me" (Psalm 51:10)!

O Pilgrim, lift your head! Come, lift your eyes to the hills, to the mountains, from where our help comes, and come with me to the Word. What does He say?

I will give you a new heart
and put a new spirit in you;
I will remove from you your heart of stone
and give you a heart of flesh.
(Ezekiel 36:26)

Do you see, Pilgrim? That deceitful, wicked heart – He has removed it! The heart out of which come evil thoughts – He has removed it and given us a new heart. To those who hear the Word of Christ and respond by believing the gospel - the glorious gospel news that whilst we were still sinners, Christ died for us, being delivered over to death for our sins and raised to life for our justification - He purifies their heart by faith (Acts 15:9). A new heart! Blessed be His Name!

Oh, but there is more, Pilgrim. Not only does He purify our hearts – He blesses those with a pure heart that they may see God. For God, who said, "Let light shine out of darkness", made His light shine in our hearts to give us the light of the knowledge of God's glory displayed in the face of Christ (2 Corinthians 4:6). When His light shines in your heart to give you the light of the knowledge of God's glory displayed in the face of Christ...you will not be able to stand in His presence. The glory of God!

40

But Pilgrim, there is still more. For He writes His law on our hearts (Jeremiah 31:33). Not just in our minds, bringing an intellectual assent – no, He writes on the fleshly tablets of our human hearts. His finger writes not with ink, but with the Spirit of the Living God (2 Corinthians 3:3). Pilgrim, this is a fiery work, painful – as He writes, you will undergo a baptism of fire. For those who are Christ's have crucified the flesh with its passions and desires (Galatians 5:24).

Pilgrim, dare you believe me when I say there is yet more? Remember we are feasting in the abundance of the house of the Lord! For He has anointed us. He has set His seal of ownership upon us (2 Corinthians 1:21-22). He has adopted us as sons. And because we are His sons, God sent the Spirit of His Son into our hearts, the Spirit who calls out, "Abba, Father" (Galatians 4:6). The Spirit is calling out! The Spirit is one who testifies, He cannot stay silent. The Spirit Himself testifies with our spirit that we are God's children (Romans 8:16). And the Spirit of truth who proceeds from the Father will testify of Jesus (John 15:26). He will glorify Jesus as He takes what is His, what is His Father's, and declares it to us (John 16:14-15). Those of us who believe in the Son of God have this testimony in us (1 John 5:10). O Pilgrim, this is not the testimony of any man - this is the testimony of God Himself concerning His Son. And this testimony is in us! In us - us who could only bring to Him our wicked, deceitful hearts....and He gives us a new heart into which He sends the Spirit of His Son calling out, "Abba, Father", testifying of Jesus, declaring to us all that is His. What a

41

truth. What a glorious truth. The riches of our inheritance! Can you believe this? It is true! The hope of glory!

O Pilgrim, when there is such a bounteous feast of abundance here, how can we respond in any way other than walking by the Spirit, that we may not grieve Him? How can we respond in any way other than by daily crucifying the flesh, and boasting in the cross of our Lord Jesus Christ, by whom the world has been crucified to us, and us to the world (Galatians 6:14)? O Pilgrim, let us encourage one another to walk in a manner worthy of the Lord. And as we continue on our path, we have this hope - that we will see God revealed in all His Glory on that day when He returns. And as we await our blessed hope, let us walk with Him on the road to Emmaus, and may our hearts burn within us as He talks with us and opens the Scriptures for us.

And this is how we know that He lives in us:
we know it by the Spirit He gave us.
(1 John 3:24)

11.
DEAR PILGRIM, HAVE YOU TASTED AND SEEN THAT THE LORD IS GOOD?

Dear Pilgrim, have you tasted and seen that the Lord is good?

Have you passed through the Valley of Eshkol? Do you recall the results of the exploration of the land of Canaan, the land of promise into which the Lord God was bringing His chosen people? Do you remember how it took two men to carry a branch bearing a single cluster of grapes from this land flowing with milk and honey (Numbers 13:23)? A single cluster of grapes, carried by two men! Oh, it was in the Valley of Eshkol, the Valley of cluster, that you first tasted and saw that the Lord is good!

You have discovered that the One you love is like an apple tree amongst the trees of the forest, and you delight to sit in His shade, for His fruit is sweet to your taste (Song of Songs 2:3). You have tasted His words, the words of the One who tasted death for you (Hebrews 2:9), and you have found them to be sweeter than honey to your mouth (Psalm 119:103). You have discovered that His fruit is better than fine gold, that what He yields surpasses choice silver (Proverbs 8:19). You have tasted that He is good, and you crave to be filled with more so that you may grow up in your salvation. You have dwelt in His garden, and you have seen that it is good. You have taken the time to browse amongst the trees and the plants in this glorious garden of His, flowing with streams of water, that have produced the choicest of fruits, foliage in abundance, richness of colour and a fragrance beyond compare. This is a garden set atop a mountain, for it is the mountains that bring prosperity to the peoples, and the hills the fruit of righteousness (Psalm 72:3). This well-watered garden has a river flowing through it which separates into four headwaters. The Pishon river gives the increase and is full-flowing. The Gihon river bursts forth and gushes through the garden. The Tigris is a swift, rapid darting river, whilst the Euphrates is sweet and fruitful. When the garden is so abundantly provided for, dear Pilgrim, is it any wonder that the fruit which comes forth from this garden is as rich and sweet as it is?

As you have delighted in His shade, your own mustard seed of faith has been planted in the fertile soil of His garden. As you have eaten with joy all He has provided for you, your roots have grown and stretched further and further into these flowing streams of life-giving water. Without your even noticing, the Vine has been wrapping itself tightly around your branches and bearing more and more fruit. For your Father is the Gardener. How He patiently tends and cares for His plants in His garden! He loves to walk in His garden in the cool of the day, examining the growth that He sees, pruning those branches which are bearing fruit that they might produce an abundance, digging around and fertilizing those trees that are not yet bearing fruit, patiently giving time for growth to occur.

He is also a Jealous Gardener. You are a garden locked-up, a spring enclosed, a sealed fountain (Song of Songs 4:12). He is Jealous that the fruit which comes from you is pure, holy and righteous, rich to the taste and lacking in no good thing. Oh, how important it is that your roots reach out to Him alone! Pilgrim, resist the temptation to seek out any other fruitless source of water, which will cause a failure to thrive and new growth to wither. Send out your roots to Him alone and you will bear the fruit of light which consists in all goodness, righteousness and truth (Ephesians 5:9). Lift up your branches for His eyes alone, not seeking the approval of men, and you will find yourself standing firm and strong before Him, an oak of righteousness, a planting of the Lord for the display of His splendour (Isaiah 61:3).

And you will find that He will breathe upon you that your fragrance might spread everywhere. For the fruit of the righteous is a tree of life, and the one who is wise saves lives (Proverbs 11:30). It is His desire that there be many plants in His garden, that it be teeming with all kinds of trees, trees that are pleasing to the eye and good to the taste, bearing the fruit of love, joy, peace, patience, kindness, goodness, faithfulness, gentleness and self-control.

For it is He who will come into His own garden and taste of its choice fruits (Song of Songs 4:16)! The One who was betrayed by a kiss in a garden will come into His own garden to gather its fruit which has faithfully been growing in Him. The One whose body was laid in a new tomb in a garden, the One who was mistaken for the gardener when He arose, He is the True Vine and His Father is the Gardener. Oh, abide in Him, dear Pilgrim! Abide in Him, and you will bear much fruit, to your Father's glory. For as the soil makes the young plant come up and a garden causes seeds to grow, so the Sovereign Lord will make righteousness and praise spring up before all nations (Isaiah 61:11).

12.
DEAR PILGRIM, WHY ARE YOUR EYES DOWNCAST?

Dear Pilgrim, why are your eyes downcast? Where is your gaze today? Under the heat of conviction of sin, are you unable to lift your eyes to heaven? Are you beating your breast, crying out to God to be merciful to you, a sinner (Luke 18:13)? Be reassured, justification is yours (Luke 18:14a).

Yet at the same time, dear Pilgrim, a great blessing awaits His people who, whilst being bowed low in His presence, have the faith to take hold of His Holy boldness to lift up their eyes before Him.

Let us consider dear Abraham, our father in the faith. The Lord Himself instructed Abraham to lift up his eyes on one occasion – and as he obeyed in faith, he saw with his own eyes the land of Promise that would one day be given to him and his descendants (Genesis 13:14-15). On another occasion when the Lord appeared to Abraham, it was only when he lifted his eyes that he saw the Lord before him (Genesis 18:2-3). His response to this was to bow low to the ground. There is no other response to the presence of the Lord. Yet this was not the end of Abraham's response. Filled with faith, he implored the Lord, "Do not pass by Your servant...let a little water be brought...wash Your feet...rest...while I bring a morsel of bread" (Genesis 18:3-5).

Do not pass me by! A cry of faith. A cry from a heart desiring intimacy. A cry from a heart that believes it is possible to fellowship with his Lord, even break bread with Him. What holy boldness! And what a response he received - not only did the Lord condescend to answer Abraham's request, He even confided in Abraham! How the Lord delighted to answer Abraham's request – because he had dared to lift his eyes.

As we lift our eyes, He reveals more of Himself to us – the awesome wonder of the work of His hands in creation (Isaiah 40:26), and the unchanging, eternal, sure word of the Lord and His attributes (Isaiah 51:6). He also uses the lifting of our eyes to reveal our sin to us (Ezekiel 8:5). Sin...without the shedding of blood there can be no forgiveness of sin. Thus Abraham lifted his eyes and saw the place where he was to offer his sacrifice to the Lord (Genesis 22:4-5), the sacrifice of his beloved son. But as Abraham lifted his eyes one final time, he set eyes on the greatest blessing of all – the ram caught in the thicket (Genesis 22:13), the Lord's own provision for the sacrifice.

Dear Pilgrim, pause a moment, and consider this – the ram, the Lord's own sacrifice, also lifted up His eyes. Listen. "He lifted up His eyes..." On whom, dear Pilgrim?

On whom did the ram, who would one day be sacrificed to take away the sin of the world, lift up His eyes? "He lifted up His eyes on His disciples..." O dear Pilgrim, listen, take heart, be encouraged, for do you know why He would lift up His eyes on His disciples?

> *"He lifted up His eyes on His disciples and said,*
> *'Blessed are you who are poor,*
> *for yours is the kingdom of God.'"*
> *(Luke 6:20)*

He lifted up His eyes on His disciples to bless them! Blessed are you who are poor! Oh, what love is this? That the One before whom we can only bow down low, and lower still as we discover the breadth and depth of His love for us, would stoop down to such a level (Luke 6:17a) that He would have to lift His eyes to us? Yes, dear Pilgrim, you who began this morning beating your breast with your gaze downcast, feeling the weight of your sin, your unworthiness before Him, He lifts up His eyes to you to bless you, for yours is the kingdom of God, for your trust and hope are in Him alone! The fulfilment of the Aaronic blessing:

> *"The Lord bless you and keep you,*
> *The Lord make His face to shine upon you*
> *and be gracious to you,*
> *The Lord lift up His countenance upon you*
> *and give you peace."*
> *(Numbers 6:24-26)*

49

Dear Pilgrim, take heart! You have His peace! Now dare to lift up your eyes to His as you bow low before Him, and He will remind you of His promises, reveal more of Himself to you, quicken you to offer yourself as a living sacrifice to Him, and reassure you that He provides all you need. And He will so fill you with Himself, that He will enable you to pray and to serve in accordance with the will of the Father, as you lift your eyes to heaven, having encountered the Living God. Dear Pilgrim, join with me in echoing Abraham's cry of faith: "Do not pass by your servant".

13.
DEAR PILGRIM, DO YOU NEED CLEANSING?

D ear Pilgrim, do you need cleansing? Is it the cry of your heart to know Him better? To enjoy a greater fullness of all that is offered through the gospel message?

Then let us consider the tabernacle in the dusty desert, the tabernacle that was outlined, with great care and in great detail, by Yahweh to Moses from the mountain top. This was the sanctuary in which the Lord would dwell among His people.

The tabernacle was located within a courtyard in the desert. White linen curtains surrounded the courtyard, symbolizing the purity of the place in which God would dwell. There was only one entrance into the courtyard, one entrance that speaks of the only way of salvation in His Name, the Name of Jesus Christ, for there is no other Name by which man might be saved. Note the colours of the curtains in the entrance – blue, purple, scarlet –

pointing to the Divine King who gave Himself as a Sacrifice.

Take note of the brazen altar. Many people came here to bring their sin offerings to the priests to be sacrificed before the Lord, that they might receive forgiveness for their sins. O Pilgrim, do you see how this bronze altar points to Him and the sacrifice that would give us the forgiveness we need for our sins? And note that there was no seat next to this altar, for the priests had to stand continually, endlessly repeating the sacrifices - as the blood from the animals could never take away sins. Take comfort, precious Pilgrim, in the knowledge that the Lamb of God sacrificed Himself for our sins once and for all, and He is now seated at the right hand of God. What a Saviour!

But dear Pilgrim, let us not fail to consider what else is in the courtyard. For our God took a great deal of care in outlining the plans for the tabernacle and its surroundings to Moses on the mountain. The courtyard was not limited to the bronze altar of sacrifice. O Pilgrim, behold, the laver (Exodus 30:17-21)!

When the pattern was given to Moses, only the priests could walk to the laver. The priests would wash themselves at the laver before entering the tabernacle so that they would not die. Pilgrim, this symbolized that in order to enter the tabernacle, the place of intimacy with the Lord, it was necessary to be clean. The Israelites could go no further than the altar, they were forbidden to enter the tabernacle. But the great truth of the sacrifice our Lord made for us is that now, He has made us all priests

(1 Peter 2:9)! Can I share with you a sorrow of my heart, Pilgrim....for so many years, I remained at the sacrificial altar, eyes cast down, not realising I was free to walk further into the tabernacle. But now He has lifted my eyes, and the laver....

For walking this Pilgrim path, it is dirty, it is dusty, and despite our best efforts our feet get dirty. Having come past the bronze altar, we have accepted His sacrifice, and we have been forgiven of our sins, hallelujah! But Pilgrim, we need washing! Our guilty consciences have been cleansed because our hearts have been sprinkled with His blood, and we have been given life that we might know Him. Yet we still need washing! Our bodies need to be washed with pure water (Hebrews 10:22)! Our feet are dirty! O Pilgrim, be cleansed!

How are we cleansed? By washing ourselves with water from the laver? This is what I tried to do for so long, my friend. It seems the right thing to do – but this is not the way of righteousness. Pilgrim, there is One who comes to clean your feet. O my friend, do we not react to this in the same way that His disciple, Simon Peter, did? "Lord, are You going to wash my feet?...You shall never wash my feet!" (John 13:6-8). Is it not enough that He had to sacrifice Himself on that cross and bear the wrath against sin in our place? Does He now have to come and bend down at our feet, our feet that need to be cleansed, take hold of them, wash them, dry them? This is not how it should be – we should be the ones to bow down at His feet. How can we let Him do this, the King of Kings?

O dear Pilgrim, allow yourself to be broken yet deeper

still. Broken in recognition of the fact that we can do nothing to cleanse ourselves of our dirt, broken from any remaining vestiges of pride, broken in recognition of the fact that the Servant King is the only One who can cleanse us, that He desires to do this for us, that it is His joy – and gratefully receive, Pilgrim! Take to heart His words, "Unless I wash you, you have no part with Me" (John 13:8). We are IN Him, through the sacrifice at the altar – to be WITH Him, to enjoy a greater fullness in our walk with Him, let Him wash us clean. Let us run to Him when our feet have become dirty, just as Peter did when he saw the risen Lord (John 21:7) - and was restored in his spirit through an intimate time of fellowship.

And after He has washed your feet clean - fall at His feet and wash them with your tears of worship.

14.
DEAR PILGRIM, HAVE YOU CLASPED
THE FEET OF JESUS?

Dear Pilgrim, have you clasped the feet of Jesus in your worship of Him? Do you recall the response of the disciples when the risen, victorious Jesus came to them and said, "Greetings!"

"They came to Him,
clasped His feet and worshipped Him."
(Matthew 28:9)

Note, they are not scrabbling in the dirt at His feet. They clasped His feet. They gripped, and clung onto, His feet. Pilgrim, have you clasped the feet of Jesus in your worship of Him?

We have a beautiful picture of this in the story of Ruth. Her mother-in-law, Naomi, said to her, "My daughter, should I not seek rest for you, that it may be well with you?" (Ruth 3:1). To find rest and provision, she pointed

Ruth to her kinsman-redeemer, and told her, "Go and uncover his feet and lie down, and he will tell you what to do" (Ruth 3:4). Uncover his feet, lie down at his feet. Dear Pilgrim, have you uncovered the feet of Jesus? Have you lain down at His uncovered feet and waited for Him to tell you what to do?

These feet....feet of which we first read in Genesis 3:15...where we find out that His heels will be bruised by Satan. We read in Psalm 22:16 that His feet will be pierced. We read in Revelation 1:15 that the feet of the risen, victorious, ascended Jesus are "like burnished bronze, refined in a furnace". Does this not remind us of the brazen altar in the tabernacle, with its grate where the fierce fire of the Lord would burn up the sacrifice to enable the worshippers to be put right with God? But remember, Pilgrim, when Korah and his two hundred and fifty followers rebelled against the Lord and brought their own incense before Him, fire came out from the Lord and consumed the two hundred and fifty men who were offering the incense. Afterwards, Eleazar the priest collected the bronze censers which had been carried by these men, for the bronze had withstood the fiery judgement of the Lord. These bronze censers were hammered out and used to overlay the altar as a reminder to the people that no-one except a descendant of Aaron could come to burn incense before the Lord (see Numbers 16:35-39). Bronze is able to withstand the Holy fires of God. Look again at the feet of Jesus – burnished bronze, refined in a furnace. Does this not all point to the cross and the way in which He suffered for our iniquities? It is because of our sin that these feet have suffered, it is because of our sin that these feet have been bruised and pierced, it is because of our sin that these feet have been through the fires of the furnace of God's wrath.

O Pilgrim, recall the woman who lived a sinful life. She learned that Jesus was eating at a Pharisee's house, so she came there with an alabaster jar of perfume (Luke 7:36-38). She stood behind Him at His feet weeping. O Pilgrim, how she loved Him! She loved Him much because she had been forgiven much. She began to wet His feet with her tears. Then she wiped them with her hair, she wiped the tears away. For He was not defeated by the sacrifice He made - look, He is robed in splendour, and strides forward in the greatness of His strength! "It is I, proclaiming victory, mighty to save!" (Isaiah 63:1). The woman replaced her tears with kisses: "Kiss the Son!" (Psalm 2:12). And then, dear Pilgrim, she poured perfume on His feet and filled the room with its beautiful fragrance. We too can pour perfume on His feet – the perfume He has given – the prayers of the Holy Spirit, who intercedes for us with groans that words cannot express – these prayers which rise like incense before Him.

Once the woman had uncovered His feet, dear Pilgrim, He spoke to her, and He told her what to do. Listen: "Your sins are forgiven…Your faith has saved you; go in peace" (Luke 7:48-50). What blessed words to hear as His feet are uncovered! Your sins are forgiven. Your faith has saved you. Salvation! Go in peace. There are no more blessed words to hear from His lips than these.

O Pilgrim, just as the woman arose and went out in peace, may His Spirit raise you to your feet, and you will find that He makes your feet like the feet of a deer, enabling you to stand on the heights. Then allow Him to put sandals on your feet that you might be ready to go forth and proclaim the gospel of peace as He wills. And you will find that the God of peace will soon crush Satan under your feet – as He must reign until He has put all His enemies under His feet, when they will become the footstool for these most precious of feet. O Pilgrim, let us exalt the Lord our God, let us worship at His footstool, for He is holy (Psalm 99:5)!

15.
DEAR PILGRIM, DARE YOU WALK BY A NEW AND LIVING WAY?

Dear Pilgrim, dare you walk by a new and living way? Do you have the confidence to enter the Most Holy Place? Will you take the opportunity to draw near to God?

It can be tempting to remain in the courtyard of the tabernacle once we have received His healing touch upon our lives. The lame man who had been begging at the Beautiful Gate made his way into the courtyard of the temple and was walking and jumping and praising God for His healing touch upon His life. The crowds were filled with wonder and amazement at what had happened to the lame man. May His Name be praised! What a wonderful Saviour is Jesus! To have our sins forgiven through the pouring out of His blood, to be washed clean in the water of His word....what more could we want? How many people have spent so much time rejoicing and exulting in the truth that they have been redeemed and they now have peace with God, that they have remained forever in the courtyard?

O dear, precious Pilgrim...there is a reason why the Lord commanded Moses to build a tabernacle. There is a reason why He gave a detailed plan to Moses of the tabernacle as He confided in him on the mountain. He was revealing the desire of His heart for His people:

"I will put My dwelling-place among you, and I will not abhor you. I will walk among you and be your God, and you will be My people. I am the Lord your God, who brought you out of Egypt so that you would no longer be slaves to the Egyptians; I broke the bars of your yoke and enabled you to walk with heads held high."
(Leviticus 26:11-13)

The Lord walked with His people in the Garden of Eden in the cool of the day – but the only time we read of this is when the heads of Adam and Eve were already held down in shame as a result of their sin and they hid from the Lord. Yet His desire is to walk among His people, His people walking with their heads held high, their fellowship with Him restored. And for those who enter through the narrow Gate of the tabernacle, who accept the sacrifice made once and for all at the bronze altar, who have their feet washed at the bronze laver, fellowship is made possible once again.

But Pilgrim, do not hold back, for in the courtyard it is not possible to experience this intimacy of relationship. Do not hold back from walking into the tabernacle by the blood of Jesus – to the place of gold! The place of deity! The place where the King Himself dwells!

The gold table of the bread of the Presence – this is where we feed on Christ Himself, the Bread of Life. "If anyone eats of this bread, he will live forever" (John 6:51). The gold lampstand – where our darkness is swept away by the One who said, "I am the light of the world. Whoever follows Me will never walk in darkness but will have the light of life" (John 8:12). The lamps were kept burning by clear olive oil, the Holy Spirit, who anoints with power. The gold altar of incense – where we offer up to the Living God our prayers and intercessions through the blood of Christ, in the Holy Spirit. And then notice the curtain torn in two from top to bottom at the far end of this room, the curtain which tore the very moment that Jesus gave up His spirit. Beyond this curtain lies the Most Holy Place.

Under the Old Covenant, only the high priest was able to enter here, and he was only able to enter the Most Holy Place on one day of the year, on the Day of Atonement, with the blood of bulls and goats. But Christ has entered the Most Holy Place once for all by His own blood, obtaining eternal redemption. Pilgrim, you now have confidence to enter the Most Holy Place by the blood of Jesus! Dare to walk into the Most Holy Place, by a new and living way – through the curtain which has been torn in two – the curtain of His body. In the Most Holy Place, the golden ark of the covenant causes us to remember that the Spirit of the living God will write upon the tablet of our hearts, provide us daily with all we need, and remind us that we have been chosen of God, and appointed to go and bear fruit that will last. The golden cherubim, wings outstretched above the mercy seat, bring to mind that this was the place where God met with Moses and spoke with him. In the Most Holy Place, as we draw near to God, our hearts having been sprinkled with the precious blood of Christ, and our bodies washed with pure water, we are free to fellowship with Him. O Pilgrim, draw near, draw near to Him!

And as you fellowship with Him, the glory of the Lord will fill the tabernacle (Exodus 40:34).

"Now the Lord is the Spirit, and where the Spirit of the Lord is, there is freedom. And we all, who with unveiled faces contemplate the Lord's glory, are being transformed into His image with ever-increasing glory, which comes from the Lord, who is the Spirit."
(2 Corinthians 3:17-18)

16.
DEAR PILGRIM, HAVE YOU SEEN HIS GLORY?

Dear Pilgrim, have you seen His glory? Just as Moses was emboldened, have you asked Him to show you His glory (Exodus 33:18)? Have you desired to see His glory?

Pilgrim, because you take delight in the Lord, He will give you the desires of your heart (Psalm 37:4). He fulfils the desires of those who fear Him (Psalm 145:19). If you desire to see His glory, this is a request He will honour.

Pilgrim, will you be bold and ask Him to show you His glory? Even though you are nothing but dust and ashes, you can be so bold as to make such a request. For your confidence does not come from yourself, but through Christ. In Christ and through faith in Him you may approach God with freedom and confidence! Will you be bold to ask Him to show you His glory?

The God who reveals Himself to those who did not ask for Him will surely delight to reveal Himself to those who desire to see His glory. This was the desire of the heart of Moses, and the Lord answered his request.

The Lord revealed His glory to Moses on the mountain (Exodus 34:2). It is on the mountains that the Lord reveals Himself! Ascend the mountain, Pilgrim, and present yourself to Him...and He will come.

But first, you must hide yourself in the cleft of the rock, dear Pilgrim, for no-one may see His face and live. This rock...my Rock, my Saviour (Psalm 18:46)! My Rock, my Redeemer (Psalm 19:14)! The Rock of our Salvation (Psalm 95:1)! Could it be that this cleft in the rock is pointing to the One who is the mediator between man and God, the man Christ Jesus?

This rock...He made water flow for His people who drank from the spiritual rock that accompanied them in the desert, that rock which was Christ (1 Corinthians 10:4). He split the rock and water gushed out (Isaiah 48:21) – and as Jesus died on the cross, a spear split His side and water gushed out (John 19:34).

This rock...this rock that makes those who do not believe fall, because they do not obey the message of salvation (1 Peter 2:8).

O Pilgrim, this cleft in the rock...it too is filled with glory! The glory of the Rock.....the glory of Christ!

For He had glory with the Father before the world began (John 17:5). When He became flesh and made His dwelling among us, His glory was seen, the glory of the Only Begotten Son (John 1:14). His glory was revealed at His birth, when the glory of the Lord shone around the shepherds in the fields nearby, and a great company of the heavenly host appeared, praising God and saying, "Glory to God in the highest!" (Luke 2:13-14). He revealed His glory when He performed the first of His miraculous signs at Cana in Galilee, when He changed water into wine (John 2:11). He was glorified when He raised Lazarus to life (John 11:4). He revealed His glory when He was transfigured on a high mountain (Luke 9:32). He will come in His glory when He returns to earth, and He will sit on His throne in heavenly glory (Matthew 25:31). He is the radiance of God's glory (Hebrews 1:3). We see the light of the knowledge of the glory of God in the face of Christ (2 Corinthians 4:6).

O Pilgrim! Is your reaction to this the same as the apostle Simon Peter who, when he had a revelation of the glory of Jesus, fell at His knees and said, "Go away from me, Lord; I am a sinful man!" (Luke 5:8). Is your reaction to this the same as the apostle John when he had a revelation of the glory of Jesus (Revelation 1:12-16): "When I saw Him, I fell at His feet as though dead" (Revelation 1:17). For when we receive a revelation of His glory, we realise how far short we have fallen of His glory. His glory reveals to us our sin. The light of His glory exposes our darkness.

Yet recall, Pilgrim, how John was not left on the ground. Remember how the Lord Jesus touched him and told him not to fear (Revelation 1:17). Remember the hope you have for the future – for that day when our bodies of sin will finally be destroyed, and as part of the bride of Christ, clothed in our glorified bodies, we will be able to sit down at the wedding feast of the Lamb, and see

Him face to face! He will raise you to your feet, to send you out to do the good works that He has prepared in advance for you to walk in, that you may be able to proclaim with David, "I have seen You in the sanctuary and beheld Your power and Your glory" (Psalm 63:2), glorifying Him with your lips. And as you go out into the darkness, where thick darkness is over the peoples, the Lord will rise upon you and His glory will appear over you (Isaiah 60:2).

17.
DEAR PILGRIM, HAS THE ROCK
POURED OUT STREAMS OF OLIVE OIL?

Dear Pilgrim, has the Rock poured out for you streams of olive oil (Job 29:6)? The Rock, whose name is like perfume poured out (Song of Songs 1:3)? Has He poured fine oils out upon you (Psalm 92:10)?

O Pilgrim, behold the Mount of Olives. The Mount of Olives, just outside of Jerusalem, a place to which the Lord Jesus was accustomed to going.

This is the mountain that David ascended barefoot, having taken off his sandals, for he knew he was standing on holy ground. David's son, Absalom, had been conspiring for some time to steal the kingdom from his father, and eventually he proclaimed himself king. Betrayed and knowing the hearts of the people had turned against him, David voluntarily left the glory of the kingdom that was rightfully his, and went up the Mount of Olives, accompanied by his friends, weeping as he went (2 Samuel 15:30). As he did so, he was foreshadowing the

Son of David who would one day come to the Mount of Olives, accompanied by His friends, as He faced betrayal from one of His closest friends, Judas. Greatly troubled and overwhelmed by sorrow, as the Son of David prayed His sweat was like drops of blood falling to the ground, in the garden of Gethsemane.

Just a few days earlier a woman had come to Him with an alabaster jar of very expensive perfume and had poured it out upon His head as He reclined at the table (Matthew 26:6-7). After she had done so, Jesus proclaimed, "When she poured this perfume on My body, she did it to prepare Me for burial" (Matthew 26:12). For He was to be poured out like water (Psalm 22:14), He was to pour out His life unto death and was to be numbered with the transgressors (Isaiah 53:12). For His blood, the blood of the new covenant, was to be poured out for many for the forgiveness of sins (Matthew 26:28).

And so as He prayed, He poured out His sweat like drops of blood falling to the ground in the garden of Gethsemane ("the oil press"). Olives were beaten from the trees, and then ground and pressed in order to extract the oil from them. Here in the garden of Gethsemane, Jesus Christ found Himself being pressed exceedingly hard as He contemplated all that was to come. Yet He was willing to endure the suffering to come for the joy that was set before Him – the anointing of the oil of joy!

For the One who had been pressed would return to the glory of the Kingdom that was rightfully His. It was from the Mount of Olives a few weeks later that the risen Lord Jesus Christ was taken up to heaven from His disciples before their very eyes, and a cloud hid Him from their sight (Acts 1:9,12). He returned to glory in order to send the oil to His own. He was the One who had declared, "The Spirit of the Lord is upon Me, for He has anointed Me to proclaim good news to the poor" (Luke 4:18). As prophets, priests and kings were anointed with oil in the Old Testament, the One who is our Prophet, Priest and King was anointed with the Holy Spirit and with power (Acts 10:38). And now exalted to the right hand of God, He has received from the Father the promised Holy Spirit, and has poured out the Spirit on His people from on high (Isaiah 32:15)!

O Pilgrim, how we need to ask Him to pour out His Spirit upon us! Let us pour our hearts out on the ground before Him as we confess our need, our desperation, for Him. Let us ask, seek, and knock that the doors of heaven might be opened and the Spirit pour down upon us. For if you then, though you are evil, know how to give good gifts to your children, how much more will your Father in heaven give the Holy Spirit to those who ask Him (Luke 11:13). May God's love be poured out into our hearts through the Holy Spirit, and may we know the blessed unity of the Spirit together, may it be like precious oil poured on the head, running down on the beard, running down on Aaron's beard, down on the collar of his robe (Psalm 133:2).

O Pilgrim, surely the Mount of Olives is holy ground! And let us remember that He will be returning again to this Mountain. For this same Jesus, who was taken into heaven, will come back in the same way (Acts 1:11). On that day His feet will stand on the Mount of Olives, east of Jerusalem, and the Mount of Olives will be split in two from east to west, forming a great valley, with half of the mountain moving north and half moving south (Zechariah 14:4). May we be ready and watching for His return.

18.
DEAR PILGRIM, HAVE YOU CALLED ON THE LORD IN YOUR DISTRESS?

Dear Pilgrim, have you called on the Lord in your distress? When trouble has come your way, have you cried out to your God for help? Have you cried out to Him for mercy as you lift up your hands to His Most Holy Place? Have you cried out to Him that He might not be deaf to your weeping? If this is so, dear Pilgrim, then you have the faith to believe that God has ears to hear.

For the idols have ears but cannot hear (Psalm 115:6) – yet it is our God Himself who fashioned the ear (Psalm 94:9)! Surely His ear is not too dull to hear (Isaiah 59:1)!

There are thunderous Holy sounds on His Holy Mountain, Pilgrim. From His throne come flashes of lightning, rumblings and peals of thunder. The seraphim above His throne call praises to one another, and at the sound of their voices the doorposts and thresholds of the temple shake. The four living creatures around the throne never stop saying, day and night, "Holy, holy, holy is the Lord God Almighty, who was, and is, and is to come" (Revelation 4:8). Whenever they move, the sound of their wings is like the roar of rushing waters, like the voice of the Almighty, like the tumult of an army. The twenty-four elders around the throne speak out their praises to Him. And the angels! O Pilgrim, there are thousands upon thousands of angels in joyful assembly, singing for joy, shouting for joy!

Pilgrim, can it be true that in such a place of Holy sounds, of Holy thunder, of Holy joy, that from His temple He hears our voices, that our cries come before Him, into His ears? Oh yes, dear Pilgrim, it is true, for our God is the God who hears! The angel of the Lord instructed Hagar to name her son Ishmael as a testament to the God who hears (Genesis 16:11)! His ears are attentive to the cry of the righteous!

Cry to Him in the morning, dear Pilgrim, lay your requests before Him and wait expectantly. Evening, morning and noon cry out in your distress, that He might hear your voice. He heard His people crying out in their captivity in Egypt, for He fulfils the desires of those who fear Him, He hears their cry and saves them (Psalm 145:19)! He will not hear the prayers of those whose iniquities separate them from their God, whose sin causes Him to hide His face from them (Isaiah 59:2). Yet when the righteous cry out, those who are walking with the Lord, who are walking before Him in humility, contrite in heart, confessing their sins, these the Lord hears. He hears the cry of His faithful servant who has been set apart for Himself (Psalm 4:3).

He heard the cries of Moses, who was faithful as a servant in all God's house. Most glorious of all, He heard Christ, who is faithful as the Son over God's house, and who was able to proclaim, "I know that You always hear Me" (John 11:42), as He brought glory to His Father during the days of His life on earth. He was heard because of His reverent submission (Hebrews 5:7). And what He Himself had heard from the One who sent Him, this He proclaimed to the world (John 8:26). He came from Heaven, and He testified of all that He had seen and heard (John 3:31-32). He returned to Heaven and has sent the Spirit to come to us, who now speaks to us only what He hears (John 16:13). And when we do not know how to pray as we should, it is He, the Spirit Himself, who intercedes for us with groanings too deep for words (Romans 8:26), which rise up before Him as fragrant incense and are heard at His throne.

For Pilgrim, it is not the loudness of our prayers that captures His attention. Our God is not one that we need to shout louder to in order to interrupt His thoughts (1 Kings 18:27). Hannah's voice could not be heard when she prayed in her heart, her lips were soundlessly moving as she poured out her soul to the Lord (1 Samuel 1:13-15). Yet the Lord heard her. He hears the needy, the one who has barely any strength to muster up the breath from within to cry out to Him, the one whose heart He has captured. When we can do no more than whisper a prayer to Him out of our distress, be reassured of this truth, dear Pilgrim - He hears, our God hears!

Let us utter these beautiful words of faith with the

prophet Micah: "My God will hear me" (Micah 7:7)! Oh, what precious faith is revealed here! Listen to the confidence! Is He your God, Pilgrim? Yes, He is, for He has called you, He has chosen you, you heard His voice calling you! Will He hear you, Pilgrim? Yes, oh yes, He will! Oh, may He give us the confidence, the assurance in Him, that no matter what situation we face, our God will hear us. May we look back at all He has done for us in the past, and remind ourselves in our present time of need that our God will hear us. May we look to Christ and how He was always heard, and know that as we cry out to our God through Christ, we too will be heard for we come in the precious name of His Son! May we be comforted that we enjoy the favour of our God, that He delights to hear our voice calling to Him, for we come through His precious Son, whose voice He always delighted to hear.

O Pilgrim, may our hearts always be inclined towards Him! May we never cease to cry out to Him! "For He says, 'In the time of My favour I heard you, and in the day of salvation I helped you.' I tell you, now is the time of God's favour, now is the day of salvation!" (2 Corinthians 6:2).

19.
DEAR PILGRIM, ARE YOU FEELING BURDENED?

Dear Pilgrim, are you feeling burdened? Are you stooped and bowing down as you struggle with the load on your back? Is the weight on your shoulders too heavy for you to carry?

There are so many things that can weigh us down as we walk the Pilgrim path, even after He removed the burden from our shoulders, when He brought us out of captivity into the land of promise. Our guilt can overwhelm us like a burden too heavy to bear (Psalm 38:4), as we forget that His blood has been sprinkled in our hearts to cleanse us from a guilty conscience. We can stumble off the narrow path, falling away from grace onto the path of legalism, trying to earn our salvation through our own works. We need reminding that it was for freedom that Christ has set us free, that we need to stand firm and not let ourselves be burdened again by a yoke of slavery (Galatians 5:1). Whilst we are in this earthly tent, our perishable earthly body, we groan and are burdened for we long to be clothed with our heavenly dwelling, so that what is mortal may be swallowed up by life (2 Corinthians 5:4).

Pilgrim, do not allow yourself to be defeated. Let us be transformed by the renewing of our minds and bring our thoughts to His Word. Let us consider something that will lift our spirits, lighten our heart and fill us with hope.

Behold Solomon's Temple. Majestic! Awesome! Bow down and worship!

Everything about this Temple points us to our Messiah. The bronze altar and bronze sea in the outer courtyard point to the sacrifices of Messiah's blood, they point to our need for washing clean in Him. Then we can enter into the Temple to meet with the Presence of the Living God, where all the golden furnishings of the temple point us to the riches of our Messiah.

But, dear Pilgrim, let us consider the pillars standing at each side of the portico of the temple (1 Kings 7:21), in the outer courtyard. One of these pillars was called "Jakin" - He establishes. The other pillar was called "Boaz" – by His strength. Dear Pilgrim, can you see – He will establish these pillars in the temple by His strength. He is building His church and the gates of hell shall not prevail against it!

O Pilgrim, as we meditate on His Word, He reveals to us further treasures. For two bronze capitals were set on the very top of the pillars. These capitals were in the shape of lilies (1 Kings 7:19). Recall that in the Song of Songs, the chosen one is called a "lily of the valleys" (Song of Songs 2:1), a lily among thorns. O Pilgrim, He is showing us that the Bridegroom has come and taken this precious lily from the depths of the valley - and where has He placed her? Right at the very peak of the pillars adorning His temple! She has made her Aliyah, her ascent! Pliny has written of the lily, "No flower grows taller; sometimes it reaches three cubits, its neck always drooping under the weight of a head too heavy for it". It is true – the lily does bow down her head for she knows she has been chosen among thorns, she knows she is what she is all through the grace of God, she knows that she has been established by His strength alone, she sees that she has been lifted up, and she can do nothing but bow down in awed wonder and worship in the presence of the Living God!

Pilgrim, He has revealed further beautiful truths about these pillars. There is a decoration of pomegranates (1 Kings 7:18) around the capital. Row upon row of pomegranates. An orchard of pomegranates! Remember what the Bridegroom says to His Beloved: "Your plants are an orchard of pomegranates with pleasant fruits" (Song of Songs 4:13). The fruit that He has caused to bear in you is an orchard of pomegranates, and this adorns the lily-shaped capital at the very peak of the pillar in His temple!

One final thought, dear Pilgrim. The capital on the pillar is usually there to mediate between the column of the pillar and the load thrusting down upon it, for normally the pillars would be supporting a heavy roof. These capitals have no load bearing down upon them. For He says to us, "My yoke is easy and my burden is light" (Matthew 11:30). O dear Pilgrim, as you bow down your head before your God, lift it up in the freedom He has given you! Just as the gates lift up their heads that the King of Glory may come in, so you too, precious lily, lift up your head, lift up your head – and the King of glory shall come in! Who is this King of Glory? Yahweh Sabaoth, the Lord of hosts, He is the King of Glory!

20.
Dear Pilgrim, are you in fear of your enemies?

Dear Pilgrim, are you in fear of your enemies? Is your heart in anguish within you? Have fear and trembling beset you?

Then the Lord has brought you to the Valley of Elah, dear Pilgrim, so that the proven genuineness of your faith – of greater worth than gold, which perishes even though refined by fire – may result in praise, glory and honour when Jesus Christ is revealed (1 Peter 1:7).

The Valley of Elah – the place where the Israelites were dismayed and terrified. For it was here that they listened to the words of the Philistine giant as he defied the armies of the living God. This was the place where the Israelites fled from their enemy in great fear whenever they saw him.

You know the story well, dear Pilgrim, you know how the young shepherd, David, came and stood against the heavily armoured Goliath with nothing more than five stones and his sling. What gave David the courage to stand against his enemy when all others were filled with terror? He knew the Name of his God, dear Pilgrim. He knew His Name.

"I come against you in the Name of the Lord of Hosts, the God of the armies of Israel, whom you have defied!"
(1 Samuel 17:45)

The Lord Almighty – Yahweh Sabaoth –the Lord of Hosts.

The Lord of Hosts, dear Pilgrim. Oh, lift up your eyes and look to the heavens: who created all these? He who brings out the starry host one by one and calls forth each of them by name. Because of His great power and mighty strength, not one of them is missing (Isaiah 40:26). He is the One who appoints the sun to shine by day, who decrees the moon and stars to shine by night, who stirs up the sea so that its waves roar – the Lord of Hosts is His Name (Jeremiah 31:35)! He is not like the images, the worthless idols which will perish when their judgement comes. He is not like these, for He is the Maker of all things, including Israel, the people of His inheritance – the Lord of Hosts is His Name (Jeremiah 10:16)! He who forms the mountains, who creates the wind, and who reveals His thoughts to mankind, who turns dawn to darkness, and treads on the heights of the earth – the Lord of Hosts is His Name (Amos 4:13)!

Pilgrim, has He revealed Himself to you as the Lord of Hosts? Have you asked Him to reveal Himself in this way to you? He will surely answer! Joshua received revelation when the Commander of the army of the Lord came and stood in front of him with a drawn sword in his hands (Joshua 5:13-14). Elisha prayed and asked for revelation for his servant, whose eyes were then opened by the Lord to see the hills full of horses and chariots of fire all around, and he finally understood that those who were with them were more than those with their enemies (2 Kings 6:16-17).

Once your eyes have been opened to see the Lord of Hosts, dear Pilgrim, they will forever reflect this encounter. Isaiah's eyes looked upon the Lord of Hosts, and it was through him that the Lord declared: "The Lord of Hosts is the One you are to regard as holy, He is the One you are to fear, He is the One you are to dread" (Isaiah 8:13). Job had heard of the Lord God, but it was after he saw the One who had laid the earth's foundations, while the morning stars sang together and all the angels shouted for joy, that he despised himself and repented in dust and ashes (Job 42:5-6).

O Pilgrim, take courage! For He is our Redeemer, the Holy One of Israel – the Lord of Hosts is His Name (Isaiah 47:4)! For the Lord of Hosts took David from the pasture, from tending the flock, and appointed him ruler over His people, Israel. He promised to establish the throne of the Son of David forever (1 Chronicles 17:7,14), and the zeal of the Lord of Hosts would accomplish this (Isaiah 9:7). When the Son of David was born at Bethlehem, a great company of the heavenly host appeared and proclaimed peace to those on whom His favour rests. Peace, Pilgrim! You have peace with the Lord of Hosts now that you are trusting in Him! Blessed is the one who trusts in the Lord of Hosts (Psalm 84:12)!

The Valley of Elah is the place where David's trust in the Name of the Lord of Hosts was proclaimed before Israel. It is the place where hearts that had been melting with fear, and hands that had been hanging limp were strengthened and encouraged as the faith of the young shepherd in his God shone brightly for all to see. It is the place where a spirit of despair was changed into garments of praise, where oaks of righteousness were a planting of the Lord for the display of His splendour. The Valley of Elah – the Valley of oaks, of strength. Be strengthened, dear Pilgrim, in the Valley of Elah!

21.
DEAR PILGRIM, WOULD YOU BE STRONG?

Dear Pilgrim, would you be strong? Would you be strong in the Lord and in His mighty power? Then first, dear Pilgrim, you must *tremble*.

Tremble as He passes by as you stand
in the cleft of the Rock,
after you ask Him to reveal His glory to you.
Worship the Lord in the splendour of His holiness and
tremble (Psalm 96:9)!
Tremble as you grasp the perfection He demands
through His law (Psalm 119:120).
Tremble at His Word, as you bow before Him, broken and
contrite in spirit (Isaiah 66:2).
Tremble at the presence of the Lord, at the presence of
the God of Jacob (Psalm 114:7)!

And then, dear Pilgrim, after He has stripped you bare

of every last ounce of self, allow Him to comfort you. Remember that He says of those who tremble before Him: "These are the ones I look on with favour" (Isaiah 66:2). Favour, Pilgrim! He looks on you with favour!

Recall His Word: "So do not fear, for I am with you; do not be dismayed, for I am your God. I will strengthen you and help you; I will uphold you with My righteous right hand" (Isaiah 41:10).

It is His righteous right hand that will uphold you and strengthen you. You see yourself as a worm, dear Pilgrim, weak and powerless – and apart from Him, this is what you are (Isaiah 41:14). But now, He has redeemed you! And it is He who will uphold you with His righteous right hand.

O Pilgrim, the voice of rejoicing and salvation can be heard in the tents of the righteous. There is a tumultuous noise of celebration! Oh, lift your voice to the heavens and join with their shouts of joy and victory! Shout out with every fibre of your being:

> *"The Lord's right hand has done mighty things (Psalm 118:16)!*
> *The Lord's right hand is lifted high (Psalm 118:16)!*
> *His right hand is victorious in power (Psalm 20:6)!*
> *His right hand has worked salvation for Him (Psalm 98:1)!*
> *His right hand is exalted (Psalm 89:13)!*
> *His right hand is majestic in power (Exodus 15:6)!*
> *His right hand is filled with righteousness (Psalm 48:10)!"*

O Pilgrim, take heart, take confidence, be strengthened by this truth, that His right hand will hold you fast, whether you are lifted high on the mountains or find yourself in the deepest valleys (Psalm 139:8-10). When His right hand holds you, His right hand which is majestic in power, no-one will be able to snatch you out of His hand – for no-one will snatch His sheep out of His hand, just as no-one can snatch His sheep out of the Father's hand (John 10:28-29). For power and might are in His hands and no-one can withstand Him. Oh, blessed truth, dear Pilgrim, what blessed comfort, when you know that you are safe in His hands!

You will discover that it is His right hand that bestows blessings upon the righteous, just as Jacob blessed the sons of Joseph by placing his right hand upon their heads. Jesus took the children in His arms, placed His hands on them and blessed them. Cling to Him, dear Pilgrim, and you will find that His right hand will uphold you as His blessing falls upon you.

So come, dear Pilgrim, and take refuge in His right hand. You will find that you are never shaken as He fills you with joy in His presence, with eternal pleasures at His right hand (Psalm 16:8-11). For these eternal pleasures, everlasting delights, this abounding joy – Pilgrim, do you see - they are to be found in the One who sits at His right hand – the One upon whom we fix our eyes, Jesus Christ, the author and perfecter of our faith, His beloved Son!

He sat down at the right hand of God, and now He waits for His enemies to be made a footstool for His feet (Hebrews 10:12-13). Exalted to the right hand of God, He received from the Father the promised Holy Spirit and has poured His Spirit out on His people (Acts 2:33). For it is His mighty power in you, which is the same as the mighty strength He exerted when He raised Christ from the dead and seated Him at His right hand in the heavenly realms (Ephesians 1:19-20), that strengthens you.

So take hold of His weapons of righteousness in your right hand and in your left hand (2 Corinthians 6:7), the shield of faith and the sword of the Spirit, which is the Word of God; put on the whole armour that He gives you, and you will stand, victorious, an overcomer in Him!

For a day is coming when His Bride, the Royal Bride, the Bride of the King of Kings, will stand at His right hand (Psalm 45:9) and He will be enthralled by her beauty.

Be strong, and take heart, all you who hope in the Lord!
(Psalm 31:24)

22.
DEAR PILGRIM, HAVE YOU BOUGHT SALVE FROM HIM?

Dear Pilgrim, have you bought salve from Him? Have you heeded His counsel to buy salve from Him to put on your eyes, that you might see clearly (Revelation 3:18)? O Pilgrim, how it is our desire to have clarity of vision, but this is a painful path to tread.

Are we not like the idols we worship – with our eyes plastered over (Isaiah 44:18) so that we cannot see? Are we not feeding on ashes, misled by a deluded heart (Isaiah 44:20), helpless to save ourselves? Are we not like the blind, groping along the wall (Isaiah 59:10), feeling our way like people without eyes, stumbling at midday as if it were twilight? Are we not walking in darkness, living in a land of deep darkness (Isaiah 9:2)?

But Pilgrim, into our world of darkness came One who reveals deep and hidden things, who knows what lies in the darkness, and in Whom light dwells (Daniel 2:22)! This One, whose Voice strikes with flashes of lightning

(Psalm 29:7), who wraps Himself in light as with a garment (Psalm 104:2a), who is the Light of the World (John 9:5), He came!

The Light came! He reached out, spat on your eyes, put His hands on you. He asked, "Do you see anything?" (Mark 8:23).

As you opened your eyes which had been released from their captivity, light rushed in to your eyes. Light! But having lived in a land of deep darkness for so long, this sudden rush of light sparked a painful reaction! The pain! Oh, the pain! The darkness....it somehow seemed more appealing than the light. The darkness...it was familiar, it was safe, it was what you knew.....the land of the shadow of death. As the light brought more sight, you saw something....but it scared you, it frightened you. You saw people walking around....yet they did not look like people. They looked like trees (Mark 8:24). You were confused, frightened, bewildered. You shut your eyes again, the sting from the light made them water, you wiped the tears from your cheeks. Denial felt safer than the truth.

You faced a choice then, dear Pilgrim. A choice to either continue to stand where you were, or to run away. You struggled as you decided whether to choose to trust Him, or to hide in the darkness. But then realization crossed your closed eyes as you whispered to yourself, "If I say, 'Surely the darkness will hide me and the light become night around me', even the darkness will not be dark to You, the night will shine like the day, for darkness is as light to You" (Psalm 139:11-12). You continued to stand where you were, holding onto a mustard seed of faith that He rewards those who earnestly seek Him.

Oh, glory! For once more He reached out and put His hands on your eyes. You felt the touch. You felt safe in His hands. You heard Him say to you, "I will lead the blind by ways they have not known, along unfamiliar paths I will guide them; I will turn the darkness into light before them and make the rough places smooth. These are the things I will do; I will not forsake them" (Isaiah 42:16). You felt safe. Safe. You dared to open your eyes again.

O precious Pilgrim! Now that your eyes were opened, and your sight was restored, you could see everything clearly (Mark 8:25)! The people no longer looked like trees walking around – they looked like people! You could see them plainly! The sting of pain had gone from your eyes! You had bought salve from Him to put on your eyes so that you might see – salve, ointment, that initially brings the sting of pain, but if only we will resist the urge to brush it away, to persevere, then He brings the comfort, the refreshing balm, the soothing touch to take away the pain, to restore sight. You allowed Him to brush away the tears from your cheek (Isaiah 25:8).

O Pilgrim, now that you can see clearly, let the light of His face shine upon you (Psalm 4:6), for you are precious and honoured in His sight. Bask in the light of His face shining upon you!

And now that you can see clearly, dear Pilgrim, He will enable you to speak out clearly too. For those who have eyes that can see clearly cannot help but speak out clearly.

Look at the example of Balaam, son of Beor, who loved the wages of wickedness (2 Peter 2:15). Even though he was being paid to speak out curses upon Israel by Balak, the King of Moab, the curse was turned into a blessing by God Almighty. For he was given clear eyes to see as the Spirit of God came upon him, and he could not help but speak out the blessing of God Almighty upon His people (Numbers 24:3,15), even when he was being paid to speak out curses. For when the eyes of those who see are no longer closed, the stammering tongue will be fluent and clear (Isaiah 32:3-4). May the message of the gospel be proclaimed clearly!

23.
DEAR PILGRIM, IS ANXIETY GREAT
WITHIN YOU?

D ear Pilgrim, is anxiety great within you (Psalm
94:19)? Are thoughts crowding into your head, as
troubles press in around you, refusing to give you any
peace?

Ah, dear Pilgrim, precious Pilgrim, the tears in your
eyes tell me that such is the weight upon you at present,
you cannot even answer. My friend, precious friend –
come, let us spend some time thinking about your walk
with Him, that His consolation might bring you joy
(Psalm 94:19) as your eyes are lifted upwards.

Remember when He led you into a field all those years
ago, and uncovered before your eyes the richest treasure
of all, the treasure of the Kingdom of God – with joy you
sold everything you had and bought that field (Matthew
13:44)! You left that field a changed person. Where you
had lived without hope before – now joy had been birthed
in your heart. Roots were laid down in the desert and the

parched land of your heart, as joy began to blossom there. With joy you took your first draught from the wells of salvation. Oh! How good the taste! Shouts of joy erupted from your soul!

As you grew in your understanding, waves of mourning swept over you, threatening to extinguish the flame of joy. As you have listened to His Words, you have wept over your own sin and the unrighteousness around you. You have mourned, precious Pilgrim. The gates of Zion lament and mourn (Isaiah 3:26). You have followed the path of wisdom and your heart has been in the house of mourning (Ecclesiastes 7:4). But you have taken comfort in these words: "The joy of the Lord is your strength" (Nehemiah 8:10). As His joy has filled you, so His comfort has flowed over.

For it is in His presence that you have come to know the fullness of joy (Psalm 16:11). It is in His presence that He has filled you with a joy unspeakable, a joy that is inexpressible and filled with glory, as He has come alongside and shown you His own wounds. His soul was overwhelmed with sorrow to the point of death as He took your sin upon His shoulders (Matthew 26:38). Yet He rejoiced over His lost sheep when He found you and joyfully put you on His shoulders (Luke 15:5). He offered up prayers and petitions with fervent cries and tears to the One who could save Him from death during the days of His life on earth (Hebrews 5:7). Yet He now rejoices over you with singing (Zephaniah 3:17). Where a crown of thorns was once cruelly set upon His head, He has now been anointed with the oil of joy (Hebrews 1:9), and it pours down His head, pours down His robes and in His presence, precious Pilgrim, it pours down upon you! O Pilgrim, draw closer to Him! Share in the oil of joy with which He has been anointed! Allow that oil of joy to pour upon your head, to seep down your collar, to drip down the robe of righteousness you are wearing. Oil travels slowly, dear Pilgrim, so take your time in His presence, do not rush away until that oil of joy covers you completely.

His Word has become a feast for you – when His words come, you eat them, for they are your joy and your heart's delight (Jeremiah 15:16). You rejoice in following His statutes as one rejoices in great riches (Psalm 119:14). Trouble and persecution come your way because of the word, yet because your roots stretch deep into Him, the enemy is unable to snatch your joy from you! For the One who endured the cross for the joy set before Him has so transformed your heart that deceit no longer dwells there, but rather you promote peace – and because of this, dear Pilgrim, you have joy (Proverbs 12:20)!

And Pilgrim, the joy He has given you has given me joy too! See how His Kingdom works! Your love has given me great joy and encouragement because you have refreshed the hearts of the Lord's people (Philemon 1:7)! My prayers for you are always filled with joy because of your partnership in the gospel from the first day until now (Philippians 1:4-5)! I rejoice when I see you because you have put your hope in His Word (Psalm 119:74)!

O Pilgrim, be encouraged, be strengthened, be heartened. It is His consolation that brings you joy at times of great anxiety. The One who comforts you – His

Spirit, the Comforter – oh! He has not left us as orphans, praise God! Draw consolation from the Comforter, lean against the breast of Jesus, pour out your concerns to Him, then allow Him to turn you to His Word, to the promise that your grief will turn to joy (John 16:20), that those who sow with tears will reap with songs of joy (Psalm 126:5), and be strengthened by Him alone.

24.
DEAR PILGRIM, DO YOU HEAR HIS VOICE?

D ear Pilgrim, do you hear His voice? Over and over again, the Scriptures confirm to us that what marks our God out as different from the idols is that whilst they "have mouths but cannot speak" (Psalm 115:5), His voice is powerful and majestic (Psalm 29:4). God merely had to speak and the heavens and the earth were created (Genesis 1:3).

If you are walking with Him today, dear Pilgrim, then you have heard Him speak, you heard Him calling you out of darkness into His wonderful light (1 Peter 2:9). For the Son of God speaks, and His words have power:

I tell you the truth, whoever hears My word and believes Him who sent Me has eternal life and will not be condemned; he has crossed over from death to life.
(John 5:24)

Those of us who have been called heard the very voice of the Son of God speaking to us! And now, as His sheep, we continue to listen to His voice (John 10:27).

God spoke to His people through Isaiah when He promised: "Whether you turn to the right or to the left, your ears will hear a voice behind you, saying, 'This is the way; walk in it'" (Isaiah 30:21). And this promise was fulfilled when He sent His Spirit. "But when He, the Spirit of truth, comes, He will guide you into all truth. He will not speak on His own; He will speak only what He hears, and He will tell you what is yet to come" (John 16:13).

Pilgrim, how blessed we are to know the comfort of the voice of the Lord, because we are obeying His voice when He said, "This is My Son whom I love; with Him I am well pleased. Listen to Him!" (Matthew 17:5). There is comfort in His voice, now that we have been delivered from the wrath of God through the One who cried out in a loud voice, "Eli, Eli, lema sabachtani" (which means 'My God, My God, why have You forsaken Me?') (Matthew 27:46). There is comfort in His voice as He intercedes for us at the right hand of God (Romans 8:34)! Comfort, dear Pilgrim!

Yet His voice is a terrible sound to those who are not resting in His salvation. The people of Israel cried out, "Let us not hear the voice of the Lord our God nor see this great fire any more, or we will die!" (Deuteronomy 18:16). He thunders with His majestic voice (Job 37:4), His voice strips the forests bare (Psalm 29:9), the earth itself melts at the sound of His voice (Psalm 46:6) when

He comes in judgment. For the Scriptures clearly declare a future time when God will speak powerfully to all people and all nations of the earth. Isaiah 63:1 tells us that when the Messiah returns to the earth, He will come "speaking in righteousness, mighty to save" on this day of vengeance.

"The Mighty One, God, the Lord, speaks and summons the earth from the rising of the sun to the place where it sets. From Zion, perfect in beauty, God shines forth. Our God comes and will not be silent; a fire devours before Him, and around Him a tempest rages. He summons the heavens above, and the earth, that He may judge His people."
(Psalm 50:1-4)

This will be a time when all people and all nations of the earth will be silenced, except for the resounding declaration when every tongue will confess that Jesus Christ is Lord, to the glory of God the Father!

And He will reign until He has put all His enemies under His feet. Pilgrim, do you recall that the last enemy to be destroyed is death (1 Corinthians 15:26)? O Pilgrim, do you know how He will destroy this last enemy? By the power of His voice! His powerful, majestic voice will speak, and death will be destroyed forever! At the sound of His voice alone, a voice full of authority, a voice that must be obeyed, the gates of death will be smashed down and destroyed! For just as He called in a loud voice to Lazarus, "Come out!" (John 11:43), so too a time is coming when all those who are in their graves will hear His voice and come out – those who have done what is good will rise to live, and those who have done what is evil will rise to be condemned (John 5:28-29).

Precious Pilgrim, you who love Him, you who walk in obedience to Him and His ways, you who bear good fruit, who walk in the good works He prepared in advance for you to do, you who trust in Him alone, do you know what you will hear His voice say to you on that great day? "Well done, good and faithful servant!" (Matthew 25:23). O Pilgrim, to those of us who love Him, who heard Him call us, His voice holds no fear, for perfect love casts out fear!

And Pilgrim, do not let your own voice be silent as you follow the voice of your Good Shepherd (John 10:4). For He cries out to you, "Let Me hear your voice!" (Song of Songs 8:13). May He hear your voice every morning (Psalm 5:3). Sing for joy on your beds (Psalm 149:5)! Shout for joy to the Lord (Psalm 100:1)! For you have come to Mount Zion, to the city of the living God, the heavenly Jerusalem. You have come to thousands upon thousands of angels in joyful assembly (Hebrews 12:22), so Pilgrim, lift up your voice and join them in hymns of praise!

25.
DEAR PILGRIM, HAVE YOU COME TO THE ANGELS IN JOYFUL ASSEMBLY?

Dear Pilgrim, have you come to the angels in joyful assembly? Have you come to the angels who are singing their praises? Have you come to the angels who are rejoicing?

For you have come to Mount Zion, to the heavenly Jerusalem, the city of the living God (Hebrews 12:22). How many angels are there, Pilgrim? There are multitudes! Thousands upon thousands of angels are there in joyful assembly! What a celebration!

You recall the great company of the heavenly host who announced the birth of Jesus into the world by praising God, and the glorious sound that was. O Pilgrim, that was a sublime taste, a precious glimpse, of the noise they are making in the city of the living God! The voice of many angels, numbering thousands upon thousands, and ten thousand times ten thousand! They are saying in a loud voice, in complete unison:

"Worthy is the Lamb, who was slain,
to receive power and wealth and wisdom and strength
and honour and glory and praise!"
(Revelation 5:12)

O Pilgrim, surely there has never been a more beautiful sound. Surely the heavens and the earth have never heard reverberations of such praise and joy and delight. Has the total absence of the sounds of mourning, of crying, of pain ever been known anywhere else?

O Pilgrim, it is the complete antithesis of the discordant notes that come from the cities of man. After Cain went out from the presence of the Lord, he began to build a city (Genesis 4:16-17), and when man builds a city, it is built on pride. The cities of man – typified by Babel. The desire to build a city, a tower, a name for man. But there is violence and strife in the city of man. Malice and abuse is within it. Destructive forces are at work in the city; threats and lies never leave its streets (Psalm 55:9-11). There is the sound of revelry and tumult in the cities of man. So the righteous judgement of the Lord confused the wicked and confounded their words. He scattered them from there over all the earth, and ever since the babbling and cacophony of the city has been a mercy of the Lord to lead sinners to repentance, for those who have ears to hear. For He will purchase with His blood those from every tribe, language, people and nation.

For we were hungry and thirsty, our lives were ebbing away. We cried out to the Lord in our trouble, and He delivered us from our distress and led us by a straight way

100

to a city where we can settle (Psalm 107:6-7). A city, not made by man, but made by God. A city with foundations, whose architect and builder is God (Hebrews 11:10). A city whose fortress is God Himself, a city that He makes secure forever. A city that is to come, yet a city that we have already come to. For we have come to Mount Zion!

O Pilgrim, do you see? Do you see that this is a city that we can already enjoy, that we can seek refuge in from all the trouble of this world – this is our City of Refuge! True, this is a city that we are looking forward to, a better country that we are longing for, for here we do not have an enduring city. We are foreigners and strangers here on earth, longing for a better country – a heavenly one. But, O Pilgrim, what glorious truth that as we look for the city that is to come, we can say at the same time that we have already come to this city of the living God! For the Lord has established Zion, and in her His afflicted people will find refuge (Isaiah 14:32).

So, dear Pilgrim, come, come to Mount Zion, to the church of the firstborn, whose names are written in heaven. Come to God, the judge of all men, to the spirits of righteous men made perfect, to Jesus the mediator of a new covenant, and to the sprinkled blood that speaks a better word than the blood of Abel (Hebrews 12:23-24). For the blood of Abel was spilt and a city was built to muffle the cry of his blood from the ground; but now the sprinkled blood grants us entrance to His City, where all cry out in praise of His blood: "Worthy is the Lamb, who was slain" (Revelation 5:12)!

O Pilgrim, God is our refuge and strength, an ever-present help in trouble. Therefore we will not fear, though the earth gives way and the mountains fall into the heart of the sea, though its waters roar and foam and the mountains quake with their surging. There is a river whose streams make glad the City of God, the Holy Place where the Most High dwells.

So come, Pilgrim, come and drink, come and quench your thirst, and be strengthened for your pilgrimage.

26.
DEAR PILGRIM,
ARE YOU THIRSTY?

Dear Pilgrim, are you thirsty? Are you feeling the burden of walking in a dry, parched land where there is no water? Is your soul thirsty? Are you like a deer, panting for some water?

Pilgrim, recall Kadesh. Forty years of wandering in the desert, witnessing the daily miraculous provision of manna from heaven, and the Israelites were thirsty. There was no water for them. Some of them must have remembered that forty years ago, when their fathers were thirsty at Horeb and grumbled, Moses cried out to God and was commanded to "strike the rock, and water will come out of it for the people to drink" (Exodus 17:6). They would have remembered that when Moses did this, water did indeed miraculously come out of the rock to satisfy their need. They would have been convicted in remembrance that Moses named the place where this had happened "Massah", which means testing – for it was the

Lord their God they were testing to see if He was among them or not. Moses also named the place "Meribah", which means quarrelling, for it was here that they had quarrelled with Moses. Forty years had passed since then, forty years in which they had been led by the Lord their God all the way through the wilderness, to humble and test them to see what was in their hearts, forty years in which He had faithfully provided for them such that their clothes never wore out, nor the sandals on their feet. Surely they would no longer act in disbelief. Surely they would turn to the living God and ask their God to quench their thirst.

Yet Pilgrim, instead of the sound of people crying out to God in humility that He might meet their need and quench their thirst, the sound of grumbling could be heard. Murmuring. They quarrelled with Moses again! Listen to what they said: "If only we had died when our brothers fell dead before the Lord! Why did you bring the Lord's community into this wilderness, that we and our livestock should die here? Why did you bring us up out of Egypt to this terrible place? It has no corn or figs, grapevines or pomegranates. And there is no water to drink!" (Numbers 20:3-5). Oh! Why were these people so stiff-necked? Why were they caught in their unbelief?

It was no wonder that Moses and Aaron went from the people and fell face down before the Lord at the entrance to the Tent of Meeting. How they must have trembled before Him, knowing that in forty years of desert wandering the Israelites were still walking without faith. The glory of the Lord appeared to them there as they interceded for the people before Him. How would the Lord respond?

The Voice of the Lord spoke to Moses and commanded him to "speak to that rock before their eyes and it will pour out its water" (Numbers 20:8). What grace! He longed to meet their need once again. Take note, Pilgrim, that Moses was commanded to speak to the rock - not strike the rock. For the Rock had been smitten once, this Rock that points us to Christ, that points us to His death once and for all for the forgiveness of sins, from whom a spring of water welling up to eternal life is given. No, this Rock had no need to be struck again. All that was needed was to "speak" to the Rock. Speak to Christ. Come before Him in humility, acknowledge your thirst, your need, your desperation for Him. It matters not that water had been given at a previous time to meet a previous thirst. The needs of today are different.

O Pilgrim, would we not expect Moses to follow the command of his God on this occasion, just as he had faithfully followed His commands throughout his walk with the Lord? But Pilgrim, he did not speak to the rock – he struck the rock twice with his rod...in frustration, in anger....disobeying the command of his God, marring the perfect picture of Christ that God had wanted to provide for His people.

But look, look at the grace of God. Water gushed out of the Rock (Numbers 20:11)! Do you see, Pilgrim? Our God has an abundant provision, and He is waiting for us to ask of Him!

O Pilgrim, behold, a high mountain! A very high

mountain in the land of Israel, to which Ezekiel was taken in a vision (Ezekiel 40:2). Pilgrim, it is from the high mountain that He reveals His abundant provision to us. Water flowed from the temple, coming out from under the threshold of the temple...it flowed from under the right side of the temple, out through the gates of the temple...and it kept flowing...as Ezekiel walked through the waters, it was ankle deep...then it was knee deep...as Ezekiel continued walking, the water came up to his waist...until eventually it was deep enough to swim in...it was too deep to cross (Ezekiel 47:3-6)! Water...water...it came gushing out of the Rock!

O Pilgrim, let us be bold, and let us ask that He might quench the thirst of our souls with the water gushing out of the Rock.

They feast on the abundance of Your house;
You give them drink from Your river of delights.
Psalm 36:8

27.
DEAR PILGRIM, DO YOU SOMETIMES
FEEL HIDDEN FROM HIS EYES?

Dear Pilgrim, do you sometimes feel hidden from His eyes? When your prayers seem to go unanswered, when your affliction weighs heavily upon you, does it seem as if His eyes are looking elsewhere? As your enemies gather around you, do you cry out in all humility, "Arise to help me; look on my plight" (Psalm 59:4)?

Pilgrim, be reassured of this truth - the eyes of the Lord are on the righteous, and His ears are attentive to their cry (Psalm 34:15). The eyes of the Lord are on those who fear Him, on those whose hope is in His unfailing love (Psalm 33:18). The eyes of the Lord range throughout the earth to strengthen those whose hearts are fully committed to Him (2 Chronicles 16:9). Woe to those who go to great depths to hide their plans from the Lord, who do their work in darkness and think, "Who sees us? Who will know?" (Isaiah 29:15). They say, "The Lord does not see; the God of Jacob takes no notice." Take notice, you senseless ones among the people; you fools, when will you become wise? Does He who fashioned the ear not hear? Does He who formed the eye not see? (Psalm 94:7-9)

For our God is unlike the idols which have eyes but cannot see (Psalm 115:5). The four living creatures surrounding the throne of God are covered with eyes, in front and behind, all round, even under their wings (Revelation 4:6,8). Covered with eyes, Pilgrim! Our God is El Roi! He sees! Our God, the One who made eyes that see, looked upon all that He had made and He declared that it was very good. And after sin had entered the world, He saw Adam and Eve hiding from Him in the Garden. He is the One who saw our unformed bodies when we were woven together in the depths of the earth. From heaven the Lord looks down and sees all mankind; from His dwelling-place He watches all who live on earth - He who forms the hearts of all, who considers everything they do (Psalm 33:13-15). Who is like the Lord our God, the One who sits enthroned on high, who stoops down to look on the heavens and the earth (Psalm 113:5-6)? The Lord looks down from heaven on all mankind to see if there are any who understand, any who seek God (Psalm 14:2).

And He has delivered His verdict – that truth is nowhere to be found, there is no justice. He saw that there was no-one, He was appalled that there was no-one to intervene (Isaiah 59:15-16). No-one, Pilgrim! Not one! O Lord, have mercy! Look on our affliction and our distress and take away all our sins (Psalm 25:18)! So His own arm achieved salvation for Him, and His own righteousness sustained Him. And people stared and gloated over Him, all who saw Him mocked Him and hurled insults at Him, they were appalled by His appearance which was disfigured beyond that of any human appearance. The One who keeps His eyes always on the Lord, the One who said He could only do what He saw His Father doing (John 5:19), His eyes closed as He died our death. But Pilgrim, He did not see decay (Psalm 16:10), for after He suffered, He saw the light of life and was satisfied (Isaiah 53:11)! What a Saviour!

And behold, our Saviour came! He came and opened our eyes to our sin, and as we looked to Him for salvation, He saw our faith and these words rang out: "Take heart, your sins are forgiven" (Matthew 9:2). And ever since, the cry of our hearts has been, "Why have I found such favour in Your eyes that You notice me?" (Ruth 2:10). It is because He sees the blood, dear Pilgrim (Exodus 12:13)! He sees the blood of His precious Son which has been sprinkled over you by faith! Listen to His declaration: "These are the ones I look on with favour: those who are humble and contrite in spirit, and who tremble at My word" (Isaiah 66:2). Be assured of your favour in His eyes as you remain bowed low before Him, submitted to Him in faith. You are not hidden from His eyes. His eyes are not looking elsewhere.

For Pilgrim, as we look at Him now, risen, ascended, glorified, His eyes are like blazing fire (Revelation 1:14). Blazing fire – eyes of love, dear Pilgrim, love for His Bride. Listen to the words of His Bride:

"Place me like a seal over Your heart,
like a seal on Your arm;
for love is as strong as death,
its jealousy unyielding as the grave.
It burns like blazing fire,
like a mighty flame."
(Song of Songs 8:6)

How He loves His Bride! How He is jealous for His Bride! O Pilgrim, His eyes of blazing fire see clearly, they burn away impurities, they expose the darkness and bring all things into the light. What eyes of love! Yet those same eyes will blaze with a holy fire on the day of His wrath when His righteous judgement is revealed. On that day those who do not know Him will cry out to the rocks and mountains to hide them from His face. Even now, Pilgrim, let us cry out to the Lord that they would see His hand lifted high, and look to Him in faith that they too would know Him as El Roi.

And may the knowledge that our God is the One who sees strengthen our faith. May this truth give us confidence and assurance in our faith to draw close to Him, to look upon Him with eyes of faith. May He lift our eyes to His that we may be blessed to see His eyes looking upon us, those eyes like blazing fire.

28.
DEAR PILGRIM, HAVE YOU TOUCHED
THE HEM OF HIS GARMENT?

Dear Pilgrim, have you touched the hem of His garment? Are you so desperate that you will push your way through the crowd pressed around Him for that touch? Do you cry out, "Whom have I in heaven but You? And earth has nothing I desire besides You!" (Psalm 73:25).

Take heart, Pilgrim, your faith will heal you as you seek His touch. Those who are not content to worship Jesus from afar, but who rather desire a personal touch from Him, oh! How He delights to bless those of such faith! For all those who touched the edge of His cloak were healed – all of them (Matthew 14:36)!

O Pilgrim, it is all too easy for us to remain in the courtyard of the tabernacle, the place where the crowds would gather. They would gather to see the Son of God perform signs and wonders, they would gather to listen to His teaching, and they would marvel at what they heard,

111

they would listen with delight. But there was widespread whispering about Him among the crowds, some saying He was a good man, others saying He deceived the people (John 7:12). It wasn't long before the crowd turned against Him and cried out for Him to be crucified.

Pilgrim, there were very few who had the courage and the faith to leave the courtyard of the tabernacle, the place where the crowds gathered, and approach the Most Holy Place – Jesus Himself. The woman with the issue of blood had the faith to approach Him. She had the faith that a touch of His garment would heal her. Yet she lacked the courage to do so publicly. She knew she was unclean, and she knew that according to the Levitical law, if she touched anyone else, they too would become unclean (Leviticus 15:19). She felt shame. She could not lift her head. So she reached out to touch Him in secrecy. She reached out to touch Him from her place within the crowd.

Maybe she didn't realise that the One she sought to touch was not a sinner like you and me who would become unclean. Rather, the One she sought to touch was Most Holy. Whatever is Most Holy does not become unclean when it is touched. Rather, whatever touches that which is Most Holy will itself become holy.

The sin offering was Most Holy (Leviticus 6:25). God made Him who had no sin to be sin for us, that in Him we might become the righteousness of God (2 Corinthians 5:21). Whatever touches any of the flesh of the sin offering becomes holy (Leviticus 6:27).

The guilt offering was Most Holy (Leviticus 6:17). He

112

sacrificed His blood for us that our hearts could be sprinkled in His blood to cleanse us from a guilty conscience (Hebrews 10:22). Whatever touches His blood becomes holy (Leviticus 6:18).

The grain offering of unleavened bread was Most Holy (Leviticus 6:17). The Bread of Life offered up His life on the cross as He became the Bread of Affliction – striped, pierced and broken. Whatever touches it becomes holy (Leviticus 6:18).

The sacred anointing oil, the fragrant blend of the perfumer, was used to anoint the tent of meeting, the ark of the covenant law, the table and all its articles, the lampstand and its accessories, the altar of incense, the altar of burnt offering and all its utensils, and the basin with its stand – all these items pointing to Christ. Consecrated by the sacred anointing oil, they all became Most Holy. What touches them becomes holy (Exodus 30:25-29). God anointed His Son with the Holy Spirit. And those of us who touch His Son have an anointing from the Holy One (1 John 2:20).

O Pilgrim! Do you see what it means to touch Him? To touch the hem of His garment? To come forward from the crowd, to seek a personal touch? What power goes out from Him! Your sin has been forgiven! Your guilty conscience has been cleansed! You have eaten of His flesh, and drunk of His blood! You have an anointing from the Holy One!

O Pilgrim, when you have acted in faith like this, you will not be able to go unnoticed (Luke 8:47). If you have approached Him in shame with your head bowed down low, have the courage to lift it up to look to the One who has met your need! And you will be given the courage to testify before the crowd, dear Pilgrim! Testify of all that He has done for you! Overcome by the word of your testimony and by the blood of the Lamb! And you will bring Him a greater glory!

Pilgrim, having touched Him, now that you have been made holy, and now that you are being made holy, just as He who called you is holy, so be holy in all you do; for it is written: "Be holy, because I am holy" (1 Peter 1:15-16).

29.
DEAR PILGRIM, HOW ARE YOU CLOTHED TODAY?

Dear Pilgrim, how are you clothed today? As you have walked this pilgrim path, He has lifted you out of a slimy pit, out of the mud and the mire; you have fallen face down before His glory; you have been made to lie down in green pastures; you have struggled against the rulers, the authorities, the powers of this dark world and against the spiritual forces of evil in the heavenly realms; you have crossed through valleys and scaled mountain peaks; you have stood on the heights. May we take a look at your garments?

O dear Pilgrim – don't hide your face in shame. Weary from your pilgrimage, you believe you are bedraggled, unkempt and stained...come, let me comfort you, I know how you feel. But take reassurance from this – that whilst the unrighteous know no shame (Zephaniah 3:5), for they do not even know how to blush (Jeremiah 6:15), it is those who are His, who know Him, who cry out, "Let us lie down in our shame, and let our disgrace cover us. We have sinned against the Lord our God, both we and our ancestors; from our youth till this day we have not obeyed the Lord our God" (Jeremiah 3:25). But Pilgrim, take this nugget of truth to heart: Blessed is the one whose transgressions are forgiven, whose sins are covered (Psalm 32:1).

For as you continue to cling to Him in repentance and belief, recognising that your own righteous deeds are as filthy rags, you do not need to worry about your clothes. Listen to His words: "See how the flowers of the field grow. They do not labour or spin. Yet I tell you that not even Solomon in all his splendour was dressed like one of these. If that is how God clothes the grass of the field, which is here today and tomorrow is thrown into the fire, will He not much more clothe you – you of little faith?" (Matthew 6:28-30).

O precious Pilgrim – how He has clothed you – but He hasn't patched up what was already there, for no-one tears a piece out of a new garment to sew on an old one (Luke 5:36). No, He has given you new garments. Jacob came dressed in the clothing of his brother (Genesis 27:15) to obtain his father's blessing. We have been dressed in the clothing of our Brother and have received the blessing of our Father. Jonathan, the son of the king, gave his royal robe to his friend, David, whom he loved (1 Samuel 18:4). The Son of God has given His royal robes to us, His friends, whom He loves. Esther, bride of the king, clothed herself in royal robes to enter the presence of the King to seek his favour (Esther 5:1). We, as the bride of the King, come clothed in royal robes to enter the presence of the King, and we are assured of His favour, for this is the Year of the Lord's favour!

Just as the father called for the best robe to be brought for the prodigal son upon his return and clothed him with it (Luke 15:22), so our Heavenly Father has called for the best robe to be brought for us to wear – He has clothed us with Christ Himself (Galatians 3:27)!

And Pilgrim, the robes in which He has clothed you are fragrant with myrrh and aloes and cassia (Psalm 45:8). This fragrance – the myrrh and cassia - does it remind you of the myrrh and cassia used in the fragrant blend of the sacred anointing oil (Exodus 30:22-25) in the tabernacle, which was poured upon Aaron, the high priest, to consecrate him for service to the Lord? This precious oil, which was poured on his head, and ran down upon the collar of his robes (Psalm 133:2-3)? The dew of Mount Zion! And what did our High Priest proclaim? "The Spirit of the Sovereign Lord is on Me, because the Lord has anointed Me to preach good news to the poor" (Isaiah 61:1). Pilgrim, do you see? The fragrant aroma – it is the Spirit of God! He has clothed us with the Spirit of God (Judges 6:34)! Is this not why Adam and Eve knew no shame when they were in the Garden of Eden, naked – for they were clothed with the Spirit of God? And in this clothing they were able to walk with Him, speak with Him, hear His Voice speaking to them! O Pilgrim, listen to His Voice speaking to you: "The fragrance of your garments is like the fragrance of Lebanon" (Song of Songs 4:11) - the beautiful fragrance of the cedars of

Lebanon! You, Pilgrim, are clothed with the Spirit of God! Take heart, Pilgrim, that as you continue to walk the pilgrim path, just as the robes of Shadrach, Meshach and Abednego were not scorched from the fiery furnace, and there was no smell of fire on them, so the fragrance of your robes will remain pure as you walk on – the power of the Spirit of God!

Come, Pilgrim – let Him take away your shame. Every last part. Show Him your wounds, your broken heart, your sin, allow Him to come and cover all of you. Ruth's kinsman-redeemer, Boaz, spread the corner of his garment over her (Ruth 3:9). Let your Kinsman-Redeemer cover every last part of you. And as you look up to Him - to Jesus, our Brother, Friend, High Priest, King - as you look to Him you will be radiant, and your face will never be covered with shame (Psalm 34:5).

30.
DEAR PILGRIM, ARE YOU SEEKING HIS FACE?

Dear Pilgrim, are you seeking His face? Does your heart say of Him, "Seek His face!" Are you looking to the Lord and His strength, are you seeking His face always?

The face of the Lord...O Pilgrim, to see His face....yes, it is true, that now we see only as a reflection in a mirror, but then, when the perfect comes, when He returns and we are gathered to Him, we will see face to face (1 Corinthians 13:12)! But the heartcry of all Pilgrims as we journey Home is that we might seek His face. And His mercy is such that He will honour the cry of His children, He will reveal glimpses of Himself to those who ask.

O Pilgrim, let us seek His face! In times of joy let us seek His face, that we may enter into something of what Moses experienced, when the Lord would speak to him face to face, as one speaks to a friend (Exodus 33:11). In times of struggle, of testing, let us seek His face, just as

119

Jacob did, and may He grant us our own Peniel (Genesis 32:30). In times of sorrow let us seek His face, just as David sought the face of the Lord when there was famine in the land for three successive years during his reign. He sought the face of the Lord – and the Lord responded by confiding in David (2 Samuel 21:1). For the Lord is righteous, He loves justice; the upright will see His face (Psalm 11:7).

To seek His face, to know His face is upon us – oh, what a sign of His favour! To find favour in the eyes of our Lord – how can this be possible? It is because we have found Christ, dear Pilgrim! "Those who find Me find life and receive favour from the Lord", cries out Wisdom (Proverbs 8:35). "These are the ones I look on with favour: those who are humble and contrite in spirit, and who tremble at My word" (Isaiah 66:2). I tell you, now is the time of God's favour (2 Corinthians 6:2). For He did not hide His face from mocking and spitting (Isaiah 50:6), rather it was we ourselves who hid our faces from Him, for we despised Him and held Him in low esteem (Isaiah 53:3). Yet He has taken away the sins that caused Him to hide His face from us (Isaiah 59:2). Oh, when He hid His face from us, how we were dismayed (Psalm 30:7). Even more – we were terrified (Psalm 104:29). But now, His face is hidden no longer, for He has poured out His Spirit upon us (Ezekiel 39:29)!

And now that we have woken up, and risen from the dead in Him, Christ shines upon us (Ephesians 5:14). The face of the Lord shines upon us! For it is from Zion, perfect in beauty, that God shines forth (Psalm 50:2). As we come to Mount Zion, as we ascend the mountain, we come closer to His brightness. It was from a high mountain that Christ was transfigured before His disciples, when His face shone like the sun (Matthew 17:2). O Pilgrim, if we would truly seek His face, let us ascend the mountain, that we may gaze upon His beauty!

Gazing upon His beauty, Pilgrim – ah, you cannot see what has happened, can you? When Moses came down from Mount Sinai with the two tablets of the covenant law in his hands, he was not aware that his face was radiant because he had spoken with the Lord (Exodus 34:29). And you, dear Pilgrim, you are not aware that your face is now radiant as you speak with the Lord! For a person's wisdom brightens their face and changes its hard appearance (Ecclesiastes 8:1), and you are gazing upon Wisdom! Those who are wise will shine like the brightness of the heavens (Daniel 12:3)! He pours His oil upon you, and it makes your face shine (Psalm 104:15), so that those who look to Him are radiant (Psalm 34:5)!

The beauty of your radiance is that you are unaware of it – for you are so caught up in gazing upon His beauty. Oh, look at what He has done here – as His face shines upon you, so your face reflects His glory, and He calls out to you…listen, dear Pilgrim, listen to what He calls out to you, as you climb the mountain to seek His face: "My dove in the clefts of the rock, in the hiding-places on the mountainside, show Me your face, let Me hear your voice; for your voice is sweet, and your face is lovely" (Song of Songs 2:14). How He wants to see your face, Pilgrim, for it brings delight and glory to Him!

121

For there is a day coming when the bride, the wife of the Lamb, the Holy City, Jerusalem, will come down out of heaven from God, shining with the glory of God, its brilliance like that of a very precious jewel, like a jasper, clear as crystal (Revelation 21:9-11), a day when His servants will see His face, when the only light will be the glory of God! Pilgrim, as we hunger and long for this glorious day, let us keep on seeking His face!

31.
DEAR PILGRIM, DO YOU REALISE YOU HAVE A RING ON YOUR FINGER?

Dear Pilgrim, do you realise you have a ring on your finger? Not only are your hands clean because He has washed you, but you also have a ring on your finger. It is a ring of royalty! How beautiful it is! It is gleaming, shining, a magnificent jewel!

Do you remember how it came to be there? You recall how you came home to your Father, hoping that He might take you in as a servant in His house, when your eyes were opened to the reality that you were eating the food of pigs. You remember when you were still a long way off, He saw you coming, ran to embrace you and kissed you. You then said to Him, "Father, I have sinned against heaven and against You and I am no longer worthy to be called Your son."

Do you remember His response? He called His servants to bring the best robe and put it on you, the robe of the Righteousness of His Son! Oh, mercy! But don't forget, He called His servants to also put a ring on your finger (Luke 15:22).

Pilgrim, take the time to consider this ring. This is a ring that confers dignity and honour. It is a ring that attests to an inheritance. Do you see? The prodigal son squandered his earthly inheritance, throwing it away in Vanity Fayre. Yet the Father gave him a ring as a sign of another inheritance, an inheritance that can never perish, spoil or fade, an inheritance in Christ.

For His Son has been appointed heir of all things (Hebrews 1:2). Just as Pharaoh took the signet ring off his own finger and gave it to Joseph as a sign that he was giving all authority to him, so too the Father has given all authority to the Son. The nations are His inheritance, the ends of the earth His possession (Psalm 2:8). When He returns, every knee will bow before Him and every tongue will confess that He is Lord.

But it is the people He redeemed with His own blood, the people of Mount Zion, who are His own inheritance (Psalm 74:2), those in whom He will be glorified when He returns! For He has given us the glory that the Father has given Him (John 17:22). "Here am I, and the children God has given me" (Hebrews 2:13). We, who have been made children of God, are His treasured possession (Malachi 3:17)! We will sparkle in His land like jewels in a crown when He returns (Zechariah 9:16)! We will shine like the brightness of the heavens, like the stars for ever and ever (Daniel 12:3)!

Furthermore dear Pilgrim – take heed – since you are His child, the Father has not only sent the Spirit of His

Son into your heart (Galatians 4:6), but He has also made you an heir (Galatians 4:7). For Christ Himself is the Signet Ring – the sign and seal of the Father – the radiance of God's glory, the exact representation of His being. And so the Spirit is the seal, the deposit guaranteeing our inheritance until the redemption of those who are God's possession. Though we were responsible for the Heir being killed, that His inheritance might be stripped of Him if that were possible (Matthew 21:38), yet in Christ we are seated with princes and inherit a throne of honour (1 Samuel 2:8)! A throne of honour! O Pilgrim! What a gospel!

This throne of honour....these words I am about to share with you, precious Pilgrim, I can hardly take them in myself. Truly, as He enlightens the eyes of our heart to know the hope to which He has called us, the riches of His glorious inheritance in the saints, this can be overwhelming. Listen, Pilgrim, to the words from His own lips: "To the one who is victorious, I will give the right to sit with Me on My throne, just as I was victorious and sat down with My Father on His throne" (Revelation 3:21). Pilgrim, I would be content to lie face down forever at His feet in His Kingdom....now I discover that He will give authority over the nations to the one who is victorious and does His will to the end, just as He received authority from His Father (Revelation 2:26).

O Pilgrim, the ring He has given you makes you an heir of God and a co-heir with Christ. This ring points to your inheritance. It points to Christ, to the seal of His Spirit in your heart. Fix your eyes on Christ. He endured the cross for the joy that was set before Him, and sat down at the right hand of the throne of God. We are co-heirs with Christ if we share in His sufferings in order that we may also share in His glory (Romans 8:16-17). If we endure we will also reign with Him (2 Timothy 2:12). For the King of Kings wore a crown of thorns to point to His Kingship, and no servant is above his Master. Yet as you endure, precious Pilgrim, remember His abundant provision of grace and the gift of righteousness that will enable you to reign in life (Romans 5:17)! It is this that will enable you to be victorious, to continue to the end, to persevere, to overcome! And remember, precious Pilgrim, that the slave woman's son will never share in the inheritance with the free woman's son (Galatians 4:30). Ask Him to enable you to walk in freedom through the grace He has given, that you may reign in life even as you share in His sufferings. You will then find that the boundary lines have fallen for you in pleasant places, that you have a delightful inheritance. And you will walk into an inheritance that is exceedingly and immeasurably beyond your comprehension.

32.
DEAR PILGRIM, ARE YOU WALKING ALONG THE STRAIGHT PATH?

Dear Pilgrim, are you walking along the straight path? Are your eyes looking straight ahead? Is your gaze fixed directly before you?

There was a time when you walked along crooked paths, paths filled with snares and pitfalls. Your feet were leading you to death, your steps were leading straight to the grave. In blindness and in darkness, you stumbled as you lurched along the twisted path, your feet were scratched, torn and bruised. Weighed down and burdened, legs shackled in chains, every step was a great effort.

Mercifully, as you travelled along this path of death, He called you. And as you saw that your life was ebbing away, you cried out to the Lord in your trouble – and He came and delivered you from your distress (Psalm 107:6)! Light shone upon you, sight was restored to your eyes – and you saw the reality of the path that you were on. You saw the pitfalls, you saw the gates of death, the deep chasm and abyss awaiting at the end of the path – and your predicament was made clear to you.

You heard a voice of one calling: "In the wilderness prepare the way for the Lord; make straight in the desert a highway for our God" (Isaiah 40:3). As the light grew in intensity around you, the chains around your legs were broken away. And you turned, dear Pilgrim...you turned around. You turned away from your sin. You turned away from the pride of your heart. You turned away from the one you had been following, when you had followed the ways of the world – the ruler of the kingdom of the air. And as you turned around, you saw that a straight road now lay ahead of you. For as you trusted in the Lord with all your heart, leaning not on your own understanding, but submitting to Him in all your ways, the path became straight before you (Proverbs 3:5-6).

As you stared in amazement at this straight path, you cast a look aside to the left and right – and at that moment you noticed you were standing at a crossroads. You stood at the crossroads and you looked. Then you asked for the ancient paths – the path of faith, of hope, of love – the good way. And you began walking in the path that was straight ahead of you.

As you took your first tentative steps, an unfamiliar feeling came flooding into your soul - peace. The way of peace you had never known before, for there had been no justice in your path. No one who walks along crooked roads knows peace (Isaiah 59:8). Yet walking along the ancient path, the straight path ahead of you – you found rest for your soul (Jeremiah 6:16). O, Pilgrim, do you understand why peace and rest for your soul are now yours? It is because this straight path leads to a city where you can settle (Psalm 107:7). But not just any city, precious Pilgrim - it is His City! Zion! His Home! Home – a place of peace, of rest! For Pilgrim, you didn't just turn around on the path – you also returned. You returned to Him, your Creator, the One who created your inmost being, who knit you together in your mother's womb, the one who made you to be with Him, to know Him, to love Him, to glorify Him! You returned to Him, your Saviour, for we had all like sheep gone astray, each of us turning to our own way – so the Lord laid on Him the iniquity of us all. You returned to Him, your King, the King of the whole earth, the King of Glory, the One to whom it is now your delight to submit. O Pilgrim, take the time to digest this beautiful truth, that when you turned on that path, you returned Home to Him.

And as you walk along the straight path, dear Pilgrim, you discover that you are not walking alone, for He is with you, He guides you along paths of righteousness for His Name's sake. As you cry out to Him to show you His ways, to teach you His paths, you realise that His Word is a lamp to your feet, a light on your path. You are encouraged as you discover that the path of the righteous is like the morning sun, shining ever brighter till the full light of day (Proverbs 4:18). As you gain understanding from His precepts, you increasingly hate every wrong path. You become more determined to keep your feet from every evil path that you might obey His Word.

Pilgrim, take heed of the warning, do not turn to the right or left as you walk. Do not allow yourself to be led astray, for many are the snares that the wicked and evildoers have set. Remain ever vigilant, with your eyes upon Him, and He will keep your feet from being ensnared. And even though the righteous may fall seven times, they will rise again (Proverbs 24:16).

As you keep on walking, continuing to look straight ahead of you, looking ahead to the City where you will settle, you discover that the path broadens out underneath your feet so that your ankles do not give way (Psalm 18:36)! You find that your feet have become so strengthened since they were released from those heavy chains, the path is now so broad, you begin to run – O Pilgrim, run, run in the path of His commands, for He has broadened your understanding (Psalm 119:32)! Run, run in the path of His commands, for He has strengthened your weak knees and feeble legs! Run, run in the path of His commands, throw off everything that hinders and the sin that so easily entangles! Run, run in the path of His commands, and you will find yourself running into His embrace!

33.
DEAR PILGRIM, HAVE YOU RECEIVED THE EMBRACE OF YOUR FATHER?

Dear Pilgrim, have you received the embrace of your Father? Have you received the comfort, the hope, the feeling of safety and the encouragement that only the warmth of His embrace can give you?

O Pilgrim, it is one thing to have been made aware that His embrace is there for you. It is another thing entirely to receive it. It is one thing to know that the love the Father has lavished on us is so great that we should be called children of God (1 John 3:1). It is another thing entirely to know that this is what you are, to have experienced the loving embrace that only a Father can give to His child. It is one thing to hear that the Father loves you because you have loved His Son and have believed that He came from God (John 16:27). It is another thing entirely to live daily in the assurance that comes from experiencing the unspeakable joy of His witness in our hearts through His Spirit.

Pilgrim, do not allow timidity to hold you back from your Father's embrace. As you approach your Father, you are coming not in your own righteousness, but clothed in the righteousness of His Son. For this is love: not that we loved God, but that He loved us and sent His Son as an atoning sacrifice for our sins (1 John 4:10). In Him and through faith in Him we may approach God with freedom and confidence (Ephesians 3:12). We have the confidence to enter the Most Holy Place by the blood of Jesus. Jacob approached his father to obtain a blessing from him, covered by his brother's robe. When his father caught the smell of his clothes, he proceeded to pour out his blessing upon his son. Pilgrim, what a picture this is for us of how we approach our heavenly Father!

Pilgrim, maybe it has been so many years since you have ever known what a father's embrace feels like, maybe you have experienced so much loss, so much heartache and pain, that you dare not come close for fear of being overwhelmed. O precious Pilgrim, let us consider Goshen.

Goshen, in Egypt – the place to which God had sent Joseph, to preserve a remnant and to save lives by a great deliverance. A place of separation from his father with whom he had enjoyed a special love, for he was the beloved son of his father. This separation had lasted many years, and had caused much pain for Joseph. But what the enemy had intended for harm, God intended for good. For we know that in all things God works for the good of those who love Him, who have been called according to His purpose (Romans 8:28). And God arranged for the beloved son to be reunited with his

132

father. As Jacob travelled to Goshen, Joseph had his chariot made ready and went to meet him. O Pilgrim, how do you think Joseph was feeling, as he went to meet his father after all those years? All those emotions flooding through him...and as he finally set eyes upon his dearly loved father, as he presented himself before his father, his emotions poured out of him and he fell on his father's neck and wept for a long time (Genesis 46:29). Oh, praise the living God for bringing about such a reconciliation!

Do you see, Pilgrim, how far the father travelled to be reconciled to his son? Jacob travelled all the way from the land of Canaan to Goshen for this reconciliation. It was not Joseph who travelled to Canaan, rather, his father came to him. O Pilgrim, do you see? Just like in the parable of the prodigal son, as soon as the son got up and went to his father, even whilst he was still a long way off, his father saw him and was filled with compassion for him. His father had been waiting, longing, for his return all those years. And as soon as he saw him, he ran to his son, threw his arms around him and kissed him (Luke 15:20)! Pilgrim, it was the father who ran to the son! Oh, what a God!

Yet, Pilgrim, it can still be possible to know all this and yet still to have not experienced it. For it requires the work of the Holy Spirit deep in our hearts, it requires God to send the Spirit of His Son into our hearts, the Spirit who calls out, "Abba, Father!" (Gal 4:6). And when this happens, dear Pilgrim, oh! The assurance He brings! The confidence He brings! The hope He brings! The warmth of His embrace is truly like no other!

May we cry out to Him that the Spirit never ceases to cry out, "Abba, Father!" from within our hearts, so that we may truly understand what it means to be a child of God, and may the Spirit Himself testify with our spirits that we are God's children (Romans 8:16). May we then be able to declare that "His right arm embraces me" (Song of Songs 2:6), and live in the confidence that this brings!

34.
DEAR PILGRIM, HAVE YOU ASKED YOUR FATHER FOR HIS GIFT?

Dear Pilgrim, have you asked your Father for His gift? Are you eagerly desiring His gifts? You have taken of the free gift of the water of life to quench your thirst (Revelation 22:17) – are you bold enough to ask for more?

O Pilgrim, behold, Mount Moriah! You are familiar with this place – where Abraham came in his time of testing, to offer his son, his only son, Isaac, the son of the promise, as a sacrifice. You are familiar with the overcoming faith as Abraham declared, "God Himself will provide the Lamb for the burnt offering, my son" (Genesis 22:8). You are familiar with the struggle as Abraham reached out his hand and took the knife to slay his son (Genesis 22:10). You are familiar with the outcome – as Abraham was told not to lay a hand on the boy, he lifted his eyes – he looked up, dear Pilgrim – and it was as he looked up that he saw the provision of his

God, the ram caught by its horns in the thicket. Jehovah-Jireh! And to this day it is said, "On the mountain of the Lord it will be provided" (Genesis 22:14).

Yes, dear Pilgrim, these words are true – on the mountain of the Lord it will be provided! He is faithful! He is the Giver of all Good Gifts!

He gave us the gift of life when He knit us together in our mother's womb. Now we are able to enjoy the beauty of His creation, however marred it may be as a result of the Fall, for it displays the invisible qualities of His eternal power and divine nature.

Every morning, He causes the sun to rise in the skies, sending its warmth and beauty into our world. He sends the rain to enable our crops to grow, whether we acknowledge Him or not. To witness the beauty of a sunset as He paints the sky myriad colours takes away the breath of those who are His children, and those who are not. We are blessed not only with hearing the birds singing His praise, but also with the senses of taste, smell and touch.

Gifts from the Giver of all Good Gifts, for every good and perfect gift is from above! How He provides! And on the mountain of the Lord, it was provided as He gave the ultimate gift on a hill called Golgotha. For God so loved the world that He gave His One and Only Son – He gave Him work to do (John 17:4), He gave Him the words to say (John 17:8), He gave Him a Name (John 17:11), He gave Him the glory (John 17:22) – and He gave Him up for us all (Romans 8:32). Oh, the grief in the Father's heart!

But Pilgrim, what a gift! What a gift He has provided! For as the Lamb of God loved us and gave Himself up for us as a fragrant offering and sacrifice to God, as He gave up His spirit, so He gave the right to become children of God to all those who received Him, to all those who believed in His Name!

Pilgrim, no truer words have been spoken than those of Naomi to her daughter-in-law Ruth, when she said to her, "My daughter, I must find a home for you, where you will be well provided for" (Ruth 3:1). The home that Ruth eventually found, in her kinsman-redeemer Boaz, points to the home we are given in our Kinsman-Redeemer, Christ Jesus. This is a home in which many rooms are provided, rooms which are filled with rare and beautiful treasures (Proverbs 24:3-4). O Pilgrim, have you asked Him to reveal these treasures to you?

For there are so many gifts awaiting to be received and unwrapped, now that we have received the gift of His Son. He who did not spare His own Son but gave Him up for us all, how will He not also, along with Him, graciously give us all things? The gift of faith (Ephesians 2:8). The gift of a new heart, a heart of flesh (Ezekiel 36:26). The gift of the Holy Spirit (Luke 11:13). The gift of eternal life (Romans 6:23). The gift of living water (John 4:10). The gift of daily bread (Matthew 6:11). The gifts of the Holy Spirit (1 Corinthians 12:4). The gift of grace (Ephesians 4:7). The gift of peace (John 14:27). The gift of righteousness (Romans 5:17). The gift of rest (Matthew 11:28). The gift of fullness in Christ (Colossians 2:10). The gift of victory (1 Corinthians 15:57)!

Let us be bold to ask Him to reveal His gifts to us, dear Pilgrim, and let us eagerly desire the spiritual gifts He has available. For on the mountain of the Lord, it will be provided. He promises to provide for all those who grieve in Zion – Zion, the mountain of the Lord (Isaiah 61:3)! He promises a crown of beauty, instead of ashes, for those who grieve in Zion. He promises the oil of joy, instead of mourning, for those who grieve in Zion. He promises a garment of praise, instead of a spirit of despair, for those who grieve in Zion.

O Pilgrim, come, come and ascend the mountain of the Lord, bring with you your grief, your grief over your sin, your grief over the dishonour of His Name in the world, your grief over those who do not know Him. Bring your grief, your contrite, broken heart, and He will provide for you. He will provide, and He will say to you, "Freely you have received; freely give" (Matthew 10:8).

35.
Dear Pilgrim, what measure are you using?

Dear Pilgrim, what measure are you using? Is it a generous helping, pressed down, shaken together and running over? Is it a full measure in response to the full measure He has poured upon you?

For He has not treated us as our sins deserve, or repaid us according to our iniquities (Psalm 103:10). For the Lord our God weighs our deeds, our motives, and our hearts – and in all cases we were weighed on the scales and we were found wanting. But where sin and wickedness increased, the grace of God increased all the more. For it was His Servant who drank the full strength of the cup of wrath, as all our sins were laid upon Him. It was He who received the full measure of all that our sins and iniquities deserved. O Pilgrim, let our tears overflow as we take in this glorious gospel truth. For He has given us not just grace and a gift through Jesus Christ – He has given us an abundant provision of grace, an abundant provision of the gift of life that we might reign in life through Jesus Christ (Romans 5:17). As Boaz poured into Ruth's shawl six measures, six whole measures, of barley when she approached her kinsman-redeemer seeking his favour (Ruth 3:15), so this points to the abundant provision that is poured into us as we approach our Kinsman-Redeemer seeking His favour.

For the grace of our Lord has been poured out on us abundantly. God is rich in mercy, and in Christ we have been given mercy in abundance (Jude 1:2). Faith, love and peace are also ours in abundance. How abundant are the good things that He has stored up for those who fear Him, that He bestows in the sight of all, on those who take refuge in Him (Psalm 31:19). Let us celebrate His abundant goodness and joyfully sing of His righteousness (Psalm 145:7)!

For it is His desire to give a full measure. Jesus wanted His disciples to have the full measure of His joy within them (John 17:13). Paul prays that the Ephesians might not only have the power to grasp the love of God, but that they would know the love of God, that they might be filled to the measure of all the fullness of God (Ephesians 3:18-19). As the fullness of the Deity lives in Christ in bodily form, so too in Christ we have been brought to fullness (Colossians 2:9-10). Listen to that again, Pilgrim – as the fullness of the Deity lives in Christ in bodily form, so too in Christ we have been brought to fullness. Fullness! O Pilgrim, are we filled with the fullness of Christ?

Just as Jesus filled the jars with water to the brim in Capernaum, so too He longs to fill us to the brim with His

140

Holy Spirit, that rivers of living water may flow from us. Let us ask Him to fill us with the Holy Spirit, that we may be filled to the brim! And as our love abounds more and more in knowledge and depth of insight, we will be filled with the fruit of righteousness that comes through Jesus Christ – for all those who hunger and thirst for righteousness will be filled. As we come to Christ, He will fill us with an inexpressible and glorious joy (1 Peter 1:8), He will fill us with all joy and peace as we trust in Him, so that we may overflow with hope by the power of the Holy Spirit (Romans 15:13). O Pilgrim, be filled, be filled to the measure of all the fullness of God!

For we worship a God who fills heaven and earth (Jeremiah 23:24). Christ descended to the lower, earthly regions, and He ascended higher than all the heavens, in order to fill the whole universe (Ephesians 4:10). And a day is coming when Israel will bud and blossom and fill the whole world with fruit (Isaiah 27:6). A day is coming when the vineyard will be fruitful, and the world will sing about it as the Lord watches over it, watering it continually. The wedding hall will be filled with guests (Matthew 22:10). It will be filled with the fragrance of perfume (John 12:3). It will be filled with His love (Psalm 119:64). It will be filled with glorious sounds of praise, coming from the mouths of those whose lips are filled with His praise, declaring His splendour all day long (Psalm 71:8). It will be filled with the glory of God.

Pilgrim, as we look for this day to come, let us ensure that we are living as children of the Most High God, using the same measure as the measure we have been given. Let us never be satisfied with anything less than a full measure! Let us love our enemies, let us show mercy, let us forgive and let us give. For whoever has will be given more, and they will have an abundance. Whoever does not have, even what they have will be taken from them (Matthew 25:29). So let us abound in every good work, for our comfort abounds in Christ.

36.
DEAR PILGRIM, DO YOU WANT TO
KNOW HIM?

Dear Pilgrim, do you want to know Him? Has He given you a heart to know Him (Jeremiah 24:7), a heart that increases in hunger and thirst for Him the more you grow in your knowledge of Him? Is your heartcry the same as that of Paul, who could confidently declare on the one hand, "I know whom I have believed" (2 Timothy 1:12), and who also yearned for more when he said, "I want to know Christ" (Philippians 3:10)?

O Pilgrim, rejoice that you do know whom you have believed! For there are some who worship what they do not know. The woman from Samaria told Jesus that her ancestors worshipped on "this mountain" (John 4:20), on Mount Gerizim. Mount Gerizim was the mountain from which the blessings were pronounced to the Israelites when they had entered the land of promise (Deuteronomy 11:29). A mountain of blessings! Abundant prosperity! The storehouse of His bounty poured out upon His people! Yet it was this mountain that became an altar of idolatry. Those who were foreigners to the covenants of promise came and settled in the land following the exile of Israel to Assyria. When they were taught how to worship the Lord, they did indeed worship Him. "But they also served their own gods in accordance with the customs of the nations from which they had been brought... Even while these people were worshipping the Lord, they were serving their idols" (2 Kings 17:33,41). And they decided that Mount Gerizim would be the mountain upon which they would worship the Lord, rather than Mount Zion.

They did not forsake all to worship the Lord. They added Him on to what they already knew. What a grievous error. The antithesis of the cry of the redeemed: "For I resolved to know nothing while I was with you except Jesus Christ and Him crucified" (1 Corinthians 2:2).

Jesus told the woman from Samaria the truth. He told her, "You Samaritans worship what you do not know" (John 4:22). What a statement! They were worshipping the Lord. They were sincere in their worship of the Lord. Yet Jesus told them they did not know Him.

O Pilgrim, let these words make us tremble. Have we forsaken all to know Him? For there are some who are always learning but never able to come to a knowledge of the truth (2 Timothy 3:7). There are some who have a form of godliness but deny its power (2 Timothy 3:5). There are some who claim to know God but by their actions they deny Him (Titus 1:16). Do we know Him?

Listen to what He says: "I am the good shepherd; I know My sheep" (John 10:14). He knows us, dear Pilgrim. We can say to Him, "You have searched me, Lord, and You know me. You know when I sit and when I rise; You perceive my thoughts from afar... Before a word is on my tongue You, Lord, know it completely... Search me, God, and know my heart; test me and know my anxious thoughts" (Psalm 139:1-2,4,23). He is the good shepherd, He knows His sheep.

But His words do not end there. "I am the good shepherd; I know My sheep and My sheep know Me – just as the Father knows Me and I know the Father" (John 10:14-15). His sheep know Him, just as the Father knows the Son and the Son knows the Father. Oh! What a wonder....that we could know Him in this same way!

And yet this is the glorious truth of the gospel message. "No longer will they teach their neighbour, or say to one another, 'Know the Lord', because they will all know Me, from the least of them to the greatest," declares the Lord (Jeremiah 31:34). "Now this is eternal life: that they know You, the only true God, and Jesus Christ, whom You have sent" (John 17:3).

How is it possible that we can know God in this way, in the same way that the Father knows the Son, in the same way that the Son knows the Father? Through His Spirit of truth. "The world cannot accept Him, because it neither sees Him nor knows Him. But you know Him, for He lives with you and will be in you" (John 14:17). "He will glorify Me because it is from Me that He will receive what He will make known to you" (John 16:14).

O Pilgrim, when the Spirit lives with us and in us, He makes known to us the Father and the Son, that we may know the Father and the Son in the same way that they know each other! This is an intimate knowing, Pilgrim. Oh, let us not be satisfied with knowing about Christ! Let us not be satisfied with knowing doctrine! For then He will speak to us as He spoke to Philip: "Don't you know Me, Philip, even after I have been among you such a long time?" (John 14:9).

Let us press on, Pilgrim. Let our hearts cry, "Seek His face!" Let us press on to know Him, just as the Father knows the Son, and the Son knows the Father. Is there any truth more precious in the whole of the gospel than this? Is there any greater love than this? Does this not bring you to your knees in awe and wonder?

"I keep asking that the
God of our Lord Jesus Christ,
the glorious Father,
may give you the Spirit of wisdom and revelation,
so that you may know Him better."
(Ephesians 1:17)

37.
DEAR PILGRIM, ARE YOU AWARE OF HOW BEAUTIFUL YOUR AROMA IS?

Dear Pilgrim, are you aware of how beautiful your aroma is? Do you realize that there is a fragrance of pleasing perfume upon you? Have you noted the delight of those who are being saved when they breathe in your aroma?

I can see from the look in your eyes, even the tears now welling in your eyes, that you are all too aware of what you perceive to be the foul stench of sin wafting around you. How you desire to be completely pure, to be free from the daily battle that corrupts and stains even the purest offering you can bring Him. How your heart trembles with sadness that even your love for Him is tainted. You think about your righteousness being like filthy rags before Him, and you are broken, emptied of self, bowed low before Him.

Dear Pilgrim, be encouraged by His Word. Listen to the voice of your Beloved:

How delightful is your love, my sister, my bride!
How much more pleasing is your love than wine, and the
fragrance of your perfume than any spice!
(Song of Songs 4:10)

O Pilgrim, what a precious truth it is that unlike
the idols which cannot smell (Psalm 115:6), Yahweh can
(Genesis 8:21)! He breathed out into the nostrils of man
His very breath, giving him life and fellowship with
Himself. And as man walked with the Lord in the Garden,
the Lord breathed in the pleasing aroma and fragrance of
fellowship with him – and He declared that it was very
good.

Sin caused a stench in the nostrils of our Holy God.
Our smell was offensive to Him, He turned His head
away. But Pilgrim, remember Golgotha! Behold, the
Lamb of God, who takes away the sins of the world!
Behold the Lamb of God, bloody, disfigured, bearing
your sin, my sin, in His body on that tree. And as you gaze
upon Your Saviour, take this truth into your heart, that
He gave Himself up for us as a fragrant offering and
sacrifice to God (Ephesians 5:2). As He hung on that
cross, He was a fragrant offering! Only the Son of God
could possibly bear all of our sin on His shoulders and at
the same time be a fragrant offering before His Father.
For this is His beloved Son, whom He loves, with Him He
is well pleased.

Precious Pilgrim, do you see? The Son is a fragrant
offering to the Father. And as you approach your Father
in the Name of His beloved Son, trusting only in Him and

in His righteousness, then the blessing of the Father falls upon you. Just as Jacob approached his father in the clothing of his brother, when the father caught the smell of his brother's clothes, he blessed him and said, "Ah, the smell of my son is like the smell of a field that the Lord has blessed" (Genesis 27:27). The fragrance of the Son is a beautiful aroma to the Father, and when He catches the smell of His Son upon us, it causes Him to exclaim in delight!

As you come before your Father through the Name of Jesus, then everything you offer your Father becomes a fragrant offering, acceptable to Him. For a good name is better than fine perfume (Ecclesiastes 7:1) and His Name is like perfume poured out (Song of Songs 1:3). So your prayers rise up as a precious, holy fragrance (Psalm 141:2) to the throne room just like the incense from the golden altar before the Ark of the Testimony in the Tabernacle. As you pray in the Spirit, with your prayers covered in the fragrant blend of sacred anointing oil, the blend of a perfumer (Exodus 30:25), He breathes in the beautiful aroma in delight. Your acts of love towards your brethren (Philippians 4:18) become a fragrant offering, an acceptable sacrifice, pleasing to God. You are to God the pleasing aroma of Christ among those who are being saved and those who are perishing (2 Corinthians 2:15).

Your aroma is also delightful to those who are being saved. It is true, to those who are perishing, your aroma brings death – for those who refuse Christ remain locked in the stench of their sins. But to those who are being saved, as they breathe in the aroma of Christ around you,

you are an aroma that brings life (2 Corinthians 2:16). You yourself have experienced this when you gather with His people, and every breath you take in is as sweet as perfume!

Ruth put on perfume as she went to lie at the feet of her kinsman-redeemer to ask him to spread the corner of his garment over her (Ruth 3:3). She wore the perfume of faith as she approached him.

And as you worship your Saviour, the Beloved Son, kneeling at His feet, pouring your heart out to Him, for Him, in adoration of who He is, all He has done and all He will yet do, the Garden is once more filled with the fragrance of perfume (John 12:3).

38.

DEAR PILGRIM, HAVE YOU NEED OF A FRIEND?

By Elizabeth DeBarros

D ear Pilgrim, are you lonely? Are you longing for some earthly comfort? Are you yearning to hear a voice that will cheer you? Do you long for a heart to confide in without reservation? Do you wish to have someone with whom you may share in the glories and sufferings of Christ?

Have you need of a friend?

Then pray, dear Pilgrim. Ask of God, and see what He might bring about! I tell you, if He can arrange the sun, moon, and stars, and by the breath of His mouth hold the galaxies in fixed array, then as surely as He did for Elijah, He can send a raven to feed the hungry (1 Kings 17:1-7). O Pilgrim, I know this to be true! He has brought me bread and meat when there was none! And how do you suppose? By coming on the wing of a friend who was at the ready, bringing me a cool drink to quench my thirsting lips long after the brook had dried up. Indeed, a true friend is one who looks after the soul of another as though it were his own.

O Pilgrim, lift your head. Cry out. Ask of Him. A friend is one of heaven's good and perfect gifts (James 1:17), and certainly your Father knows how to give such. He knows what you have need of even before you ask (Matthew 6:7-8)!

Will you trust Him?

For though it is good to pray, thereafter one must trust God, even when the answer seems delayed in coming. He will answer in due time, revealing at once His omniscience and omnibenevolence. O my dear Pilgrim, never let there be a doubt in how He cares for your soul. He delights to make Himself known to you through the blessed goodwill of a friend. Wait on Him.

Now, may I offer you some further earnest counsel?

It is not unusual to long for a companion, someone with whom to walk alongside on this world-weary, dust-laden trail. Heaven knows the birds do not talk back, and though the winds may murmur and moan, they faithfully return back to the hollow. Surely the limbs grow stiff without the gentle stoking of a willing companion with whom to walk apace (Proverbs 27:9)! But gems are rare, and they are even harder to find. After years of searching, one can take solace in hermitage. But before long, that one suffers blight. Like a withering flower, the soul grows forlorn from a lack of sun and rain. Parchedness takes over and spiritual malaise sets in. The heart hardens. And then a peculiar sort of soul-sickness develops into black coldness. Beware of this temptation. Do not allow such bereavement to gain dominion. It will be a cancer for which there is no cure! You must keep your heart ever tender, ever yearning, ever believing that God knows what you have need of, and He takes the best of care. In due time, He will richly supply you with fellowship sent from on high. Watch for Him.

Yet, even so, another thing comes to mind, dear Pilgrim. May I ask you another question?

Could it be, in this lonely time, that God might want you all to Himself? Pause and consider for a moment. Does not your Father have the right to draw you aside, bring you into His chamber, to teach you what it means to lean on the arm of no man save His own? This, too, is a faithful wound (Proverbs 27:6), one that yields strength and courage for those dark, wintry nights of the soul. I urge you, find in Him this friend, one who sticks closer than a brother (Proverbs 18:24), and your journey will lighten, the road will open up, the mountains and the hills shall break forth into singing and all the trees of the field shall clap their hands (Isaiah 55:12).

O Pilgrim, truly He is your All in all. But to have someone like you — yet different — someone with whom to walk along the road is indeed among the best of all earthly joys. To have a friend to lean on in times of trouble, a confidant with whom to reveal old scars and fresh wounds, this is, most assuredly, a heavenly gift! It is as though a sunbeam has been appointed to shine downward upon you, like the sending of good news from another country altogether (Proverbs 25:25)! It is the tall glass of water men thirst for! A genuine friend is one who fulfils the order tenfold.

Dear Pilgrim, at last, may I remind you of this: when He sends a friend to bless, there is no trouble added (Proverbs 10:22). It is a spiritual blessing that has come at a price, the precious blood of Christ. To this is owed the unity of hearts and minds in the tender graces and mercies of the Holy Spirit. Such a heavenly bond is uniquely reserved for His saints, wherein abides a mutual affection and whence the God of endurance and encouragement dwells (Romans 15:5-6). Ask Him, O Pilgrim, for this kind of friend. Soon you will be drinking from a cup that holds the very dew of heaven.

39.
DEAR PILGRIM, HAS HE BAPTISED YOU WITH FIRE?

Dear Pilgrim, has He baptised you with fire? He came not only to baptise with the Holy Spirit, but to baptise with fire. Have you experienced the fire of His baptism?

For the Lord our God is a consuming fire. His voice spoke out of the fire with which He set Mount Sinai ablaze, and terrified the people of Israel. Ezekiel saw a vision of the likeness of the glory of God. He saw high above on the throne a figure like that of a man, who from His waist up looked like glowing metal, as if full of fire, and from there down He looked like fire (Ezekiel 1:27). Daniel saw a vision of the Ancient of Days. His throne was flaming with fire, its wheels were all ablaze, whilst a river of fire was flowing, coming out from before Him (Daniel 7:9-10). O Pilgrim, our God is a consuming fire!

He is a God who answers by fire. He answered by fire when Elijah called out to Him from Mount Carmel that the people might know He was the God of Israel. The fire of the Lord fell and burned up the sacrifice, the wood, the stones, the soil, which were all drenched in water (1 Kings 18:36-38), for He makes flames of fire His servants.

He is a God whose fire burns amongst His people. O Pilgrim, remember Taberah – the place of burning. Recall the Israelites, redeemed out of the hands of their enemies, brought to the wilderness. They had just left the base of Mount Sinai from where God had been speaking to them out of the fire, and just three days into their journey to the promised land, they complained of their hardships. O Pilgrim, He heard their complaining and it aroused His anger. Recall how fire from the Lord came and burned among them and consumed some of the outskirts of their camp. How did the people respond? They cried out to Moses, who cried out to the Lord – and the fire died down (Numbers 11:1-3).

O Pilgrim, what a picture, what a picture for us of Christ. Yet first, He had a baptism of His own to undergo. For the wrath of God burns like fire against all sin, and so the Passover Lamb, the Lamb of God, was roasted over a fire of wrath as He Himself bore our sins in His body on the cross. But just as the bush did not burn up even though it was on fire, just as the four men in the blazing furnace were untouched by the flames, so our Lamb of God was not consumed by the fiery furnace of wrath, but emerged triumphant and victorious from the grave! And now we can cry out to Jesus to deliver us from the fires of the wrath of God!

Saved from the fires of the wrath of God – yet everyone

will be salted with fire (Mark 9:49). Now that we have been saved from the fires of His wrath, what is this fire with which we will be salted? Pilgrim, is it not the fires of His jealousy? For He says, "I am very jealous for Zion; I am burning with jealousy for her" (Zechariah 8:2). The Bride calls out to her beloved, "Place me like a seal over Your heart, like a seal on Your arm; for love is as strong as death, its jealousy unyielding as the grave. It burns like blazing fire, like a mighty flame" (Song of Songs 8:6). For we have been promised to one husband, Christ, and we are to be presented as a pure virgin to Him. So the Lord will wash away the filth from Zion; He will cleanse the bloodstains from Jerusalem by a spirit of judgment and a spirit of fire.

O Pilgrim, would you return to the Garden of Eden, the Garden on the mountain from which man fell? Would you return to the Garden that He planted, that you may walk with Him, in unity with Him? Then you must walk through the flaming sword that flashes back and forth guarding the way to the tree of life (Genesis 3:24). The flaming sword fell on Him as He died our death, paying the penalty for our sin. We must also walk through the flaming sword, the sword of fire, as we die with Him that we may also live with Him.

Come, Pilgrim, come to the refiner's fire! For after He provided the sacrifice for our sins, He sat down at the right hand of God, and now He sits as a refiner and purifier of silver, as He refines us like gold and silver (Malachi 3:2-3). He sits, paying careful, unhurried attention to His task, as all the impurities are burned away through the grief we may have had to suffer in all kinds of trials, that we might better reflect His glory. He counsels us to come and buy from Him gold refined in the fire, that we might become rich. Take heart from His words of comfort to us, that when we walk through the fire, we will not be burned; the flames will not set us ablaze, for He will be with us (Isaiah 43:2). O Pilgrim, rejoice that He would take such care and attention over His Bride, that we might be found spotless, blameless and at peace with Him when He returns in blazing fire!

For it is only as incense is burned that its fragrance rises as a pleasing aroma. It is only as the oil in the lamp burns that the light shines in the darkness. It is He who keeps our lamps burning, it is He who keeps the incense burning. And as His Word burns like fire, we will find that our hearts burn within us as our Refiner talks with us and opens the Scriptures to us.

40.
DEAR PILGRIM, ARE YOU IN TIMES OF TROUBLE?

Dear Pilgrim, are you in times of trouble? Are difficulties and concerns crowding in around you? Are you feeling oppressed and afflicted?

Then lift your head, dear Pilgrim, for we worship the Father of compassion and the God of all comfort, who comforts us in all our troubles, so that we can comfort those in any trouble with the comfort we ourselves receive from God (2 Corinthians 1:3-4). God is our refuge and strength, an ever-present help in trouble (Psalm 46:1). The righteous person may have many troubles, but the Lord delivers him from them all (Psalm 34:19). What a testimony! He will deliver you from all your troubles, dear Pilgrim!

How is this possible? Through Christ! Listen to His words: "In this world you will have trouble. But take heart! I have overcome the world!" (John 16:33).

Though trouble comes our way, He has overcome the

159

world. He has won the victory! It is finished! For it is His desire that though we walk in the midst of trouble, yet in Him we have peace (John 16:33). Peace with God! O why, my soul, are you downcast? Why so disturbed within me? Put your hope in God, for I will yet praise Him, my Saviour and my God. My Saviour and my God! Our Saviour and our God, dear Pilgrim! He has saved us out of our trouble!

How He has saved us, dear Pilgrim! Behold, the Valley of Achor (Joshua 7:26) – the valley of trouble. Oh, what a wretched place this is. The site of Achan's sin against God. The place where Achan stole from God, and lied to God, in a vain attempt to cover up what he had done. But nothing is hidden from the eyes of God, and He saw. Achan's sin was uncovered by God. Achan was revealed to be the one who had brought trouble upon Israel because of his sin. And trouble came upon him that day as he was stoned to death because of his sin in the Valley of Achor, the valley of trouble.

O Pilgrim, does this not cause us to tremble? For are we not troubled by our sin? There is no one who is good, not one. Are we not as guilty as Achan? Do we not cry out with the Psalmist, "...troubles without number surround me; my sins have overtaken me, and I cannot see. They are more than the hairs of my head, and my heart fails within me" (Psalm 40:12).

O Pilgrim, take heart, be encouraged, for in the Valley of Achor, a door is appearing in the midst of this valley of trouble! A door! It is a door of olive wood (1 Kings 6:31). Olive wood....the olive tree which has been beaten for its fruit (Isaiah 24:13), and is now stripped bare for all to stare at. O Pilgrim, the symbolism is impossible to ignore. This door is His cross – the cross where all of the trouble of sin, all of it, fell upon His shoulders as He died the death that should have been ours. The trouble of sin that fell upon Him was so great that darkness fell across the land for three hours. As He breathed His last breath, it appeared that all hope was gone. But that would be to ignore His last words: "It is finished!" For three days later, the trouble of sin was transformed into a door of hope, as He rose triumphant from the grave, opening up a new and living Way to enter the Most Holy Place, through this Door of Hope, Jesus Christ. For He said, "I am the door" (John 10:9). Christ Jesus, our hope, is the narrow Door leading to the Most Holy Place, and it is this narrow Door that we must enter through! So let us make every effort to enter through the narrow door, for many will try to enter and will not be able to (Luke 13:24). Let us ask, seek and knock that the Door may be opened for us (Matthew 7:7).

O Pilgrim, He promised that He would make the Valley of Achor a Door of Hope (Hosea 2:15). He promised that the Valley of Achor would become a resting-place for herds (Isaiah 65:10). And no matter how many promises God has made, they are "Yes" in Christ! As we pass through the Door of Hope, we are delivered from our troubles of sin, and we walk into His promised rest in Christ. As we pass through the Door of Hope, may we not be like King Ahaz, who in his time of trouble became even more unfaithful to the Lord (2 Chronicles

28:22). Rather, may we be like Paul, who in his time of trouble made his good confession of faith, saying, "This happened that we might not rely on ourselves but on God, who raises the dead" (2 Corinthians 1:9). O Pilgrim, let us hold unswervingly to the hope we profess, for He who promised is faithful! It is our hope in our Lord Jesus Christ that will inspire us to endure. Let us set our hope on Him alone, and as we do so, dear Pilgrim, may the God of hope fill us with all joy and peace as we trust in Him, so that we may overflow with hope by the power of the Holy Spirit (Romans 15:13).

41.
DEAR PILGRIM, ARE YOU EXHAUSTED FROM THE BATTLE?

Dear Pilgrim, are you exhausted from the battle? Is your heart faint within you? Do your eyes grow weak with sorrow, your soul and body weak with grief?

O Pilgrim, let us call to mind the events at Besor Brook, that you may be encouraged in your time of need. Besor Brook was not far from Ziklag, where a scene of utter devastation met David and his men as they returned from battle. It had taken them three days to return home where they had hoped to be reunited with their families. But instead they found their home town had been attacked by Amalekites in their absence. It was utterly destroyed by fire. It was decimated. Not only had they lost their homes, but to their horror they discovered their wives, sons and daughters had been taken captive by the Amalekites.

David and his men wept aloud until they had no strength left to weep (1 Samuel 30:4). Whereas his men became bitter in their distress, David strengthened himself in the Lord his God. O Pilgrim, whenever we face times of testing and trials, may we follow the example of David, may we strengthen ourselves in the Lord our God!

Having been strengthened, David enquired of the Lord and received an assurance that he and his men would have success in rescuing their loved ones from the hand of the enemy. So David and his six hundred men set out in pursuit.

They travelled many miles to the Besor Brook, but it was at this point that two hundred of David's men were too exhausted to go any further. They saw the valley before them which had to be crossed, and their strength failed them. They were in desperate need of spiritual, mental and physical refreshment and could go no further. So they stayed with the supplies, whilst David and his four hundred men continued the pursuit.

The Lord led them down to the Amalekites who were by now scattered over the countryside. Praise be to the living God, for in His grace He granted David and the four hundred men victory in battle with the Amalekites, and they recovered everything that had been taken – all their loved ones, all their livestock, all that had been plundered! With great joy and delight they retraced their steps and rejoined the two hundred who were faithfully waiting for them at the Besor Brook.

David, full of compassion, asked the two hundred how they were (1 Samuel 30:21). He was greatly concerned for them. For he knew his God. He knew that as a father has compassion on his children, so the Lord has compassion on those who fear Him; for He knows how we are formed, He remembers that we are dust (Psalm 103:13-14). And so, like the Son of David to come, his heart went out to his people.

But within the company of his people, tares were growing up among the wheat. All the evil men and troublemakers among David's followers said, "Because they did not go out with us, we will not share with them the plunder we recovered. However, each man may take his wife and children and go" (1 Samuel 30:22).

Oh! How the strong had no regard for the weak! For those parts of the body that seem weaker are indispensable (1 Corinthians 12:22)! For God has put the body together, giving greater honour to the parts that lacked it, so that there should be no division in the body, but that its parts should have equal concern for each other. If one part suffers, every part suffers with it; if one part is honoured, every part rejoices with it (1 Corinthians 12:24-26).

The Lord has a word for those sheep who believe they are strong. "See, I Myself will judge between the fat sheep and the lean sheep. Because you shove with flank and shoulder, butting all the weak sheep with your horns until you have driven them away, I will save My flock, and they will no longer be plundered. I will judge between one sheep and another. I will place over them one shepherd, My servant David, and He will tend them; He will tend them and be their shepherd" (Ezekiel 34:20-23).

And His servant David, speaking for the Son of David to come, said to those of his men who saw themselves as strong, "No, my brothers, you must not do that with what the Lord has given us. He has protected us and delivered into our hands the raiding party that came against us. Who will listen to what you say? The share of the man who stayed with the supplies is to be the same as that of him who went down to the battle. All shall share alike" (1 Samuel 30:23-24).

Grace. Words of grace. He recognised that the Lord had been merciful to them in granting them success in the battle with the Amalekites. And so he himself was willing to show mercy to those who had been too exhausted to join with them. Blessed are the merciful, for they shall be shown mercy! Blessed are those who have regard for the weak; the Lord delivers them in times of trouble (Psalm 41:1)!

For the Son of David will not break a bruised reed, or snuff out a smouldering wick (Isaiah 42:3). Instead, He gives strength to the weary, and increases the power of the weak (Isaiah 40:29). Those who hope in the Lord will renew their strength. They will soar on wings like eagles; they will run and not grow weary, they will walk and not be faint (Isaiah 40:31). For He gives abundant showers; He refreshes His weary inheritance (Psalm 68:9).

42.
DEAR PILGRIM, IS HE YOUR SONG IN THE NIGHT?

D ear Pilgrim, is He your song in the night? Is He the theme of your song both by day and by night? Your spirit longs for Him in the morning – does your soul yearn for Him in the night?

O Pilgrim, how our heart rejoices to sing His praise in response to His great deliverance, in the light of the day! Dawn breaks forth across the land, sending the darkness and shadows scurrying away, and just like Miriam, we take our tambourines and dance before the Lord - "My lips will shout for joy when I sing praise to You – I whom You have delivered" (Psalm 71:23). Just like David, we sing the words of our song when the Lord has delivered us from the hand of our enemies (2 Samuel 22:1). Just like Deborah, we sing a new song to Him in praise of the marvellous things He has done. The songs of the day are glorious! With His light shining on all His creation, the sea resounds and everything in it, the rivers clap their hands, and the mountains sing for joy! Oh, shout for joy all the earth!

Pilgrim, when the evening fades, when darkness closes in, when the terrors of the night come along and your enemies are gathered against you, can your soul still find it within you to sing His praise? Do the songs of Zion continue to tumble from your lips? Or are the joyful tambourines stilled, is the joyful harp silent?

O Pilgrim, let me offer you this encouragement for those times of darkness – it is not you who has to find this song from within. For listen to this great truth – God your Maker is the One who gives songs in the night (Job 35:10)! By day the Lord directs His love – at night His song is with you (Psalm 42:8)! He is the One who will give you a song to sing at this time of great darkness. For it is He who instructed the temple musicians to be responsible for their work both by day and by night (1 Chronicles 9:33). And as the servants of the Lord ministered by night in the house of the Lord, lifting up their hands in the sanctuary and praising the Lord, He blessed them from Zion (Psalm 134)! The Maker of heaven and earth blessed them from Zion with songs from Zion!

The people of Judah gathered before the Lord at a time of darkness – as a vast army approached them. King Jehoshaphat called out to the Lord from within the darkness: "We have no power to face this vast enemy that is attacking us. We do not know what to do, but our eyes are upon You." All the men of Judah, with their wives and children and little ones, stood there before the Lord (2 Chronicles 20:12-13). The Spirit of the Lord spoke to a

168

descendant of Asaph, whom David had appointed to lead the praise of the Lord (1 Chronicles 16:5), encouraging them to go and face their enemies, "for the battle is not yours, but God's" (2 Chronicles 20:15). As they headed out to meet their enemies, Jehoshaphat appointed men to sing to the Lord and to praise Him for the splendour of His holiness as they went out at the head of the army. God their Maker gave them songs in the night. And as they began to sing and praise, the Lord set ambushes against their enemies (2 Chronicles 20:21-22).

Paul and Silas had been severely flogged and thrown into prison, for they had been counted worthy of suffering for the gospel. God their Maker gave them songs in the night. And about midnight, as they prayed and sang hymns to the Lord, a violent earthquake shook the foundations of the prison and loosened their chains (Acts 16:25-26)!

O Pilgrim, think of Him through the watches of the night, meditate on His promises as your eyes stay open through the watches of the night, and as He comes alongside you in the darkness, sing in the shadow of His wings (Psalm 63:6-7)! As He draws near to you, so near that you reach out and cling to Him, sing for joy on your bed! May the praise of God be in your mouth and a double-edged sword in your hands (Psalm 149:5-6). For as you sing and make music from your heart to the Lord, as you sing psalms, hymns and songs from the Spirit (Ephesians 5:19), you are holding a sword in your hands (Ephesians 6:17). And He will use this sword to defeat your enemies – for "not by might, nor by power, but by

My Spirit" says the Lord of Hosts (Zechariah 4:6). The darkness will pass, and the light will return.

O Pilgrim, sing praises to the Lord! Sing praises in the Valley of Berakah, in the Valley of Praise (2 Chronicles 20:26)! The whole earth is filled with awe at His wonders, for where morning dawns, and where evening fades, He calls forth songs of joy (Psalm 65:8)!

43.

DEAR PILGRIM, HAVE YOU CRIED OUT TO HIM TO LIFT YOU UP?

Dear Pilgrim, have you cried out to Him to lift you up? When you have found yourself in a pit, a pit which is dark and caked in mud, have you lifted your eyes to Him? Have you lifted your hands to the One who can lift you up?

For Pilgrim, there are times when the burden we carry feels like it will crush us. Under its weight we stoop and bow down, unable to find release. The burden of guilt can overwhelm us, for it is a burden too heavy to bear, whilst the burden of the yoke of slavery is intense, dragging us to our knees in despair and anguish. As our knees buckle under us, our feet stumble over the side of the dark pit which is waiting to receive us.

There are times when we can only cry out to God, "I am too ashamed and disgraced, my God, to lift up my face to You, because my sin is higher than my head and my guilt has reached to the heavens" (Ezra 9:6). Times when we have made a choice to wander off the narrow path of life and onto the broad path to destruction. Times when we have followed the blind. And when the blind lead the blind, they will both fall into a pit.

There are times when we can be so overwhelmed by troubles, when persecution comes our way, when friends desert us, when all strength evaporates from us, that it seems as though He has hidden His face from us as we are cast into the darkest depths of the pit.

O Pilgrim, how dark the pit is, how slimy the walls, with feet encased in mud, and no way of escape. This is a place where the flames of hope, which once burned fiercely in your heart, are suddenly extinguished, snuffed out like a wick. This is a place where darkness seems to be your closest friend, where the cold fingers of despair weave their way around your heart, where the icy arms of depression welcome you into their embrace.

Pilgrim, all is not lost! Hope is not lost! Lift your eyes, dear Pilgrim! Lift your eyes to the mountains! Where does your help come from? Your help comes from the Lord, the Maker of heaven and earth! He is your Creator! The One who created you, the One who redeems your life from the pit.

For the One who is exalted was Himself lifted up from the earth. Just as Moses lifted up the snake in the wilderness, so the Son of Man was lifted up, that He might draw all men to Himself. Just as Moses lifted up the bronze snake that all who looked to it might live, so the Son of Man was lifted up that all who look to Him might live.

Pilgrim, lift your eyes to Him, lift your hands to Him, lift your voice to Him, cry to Him for mercy! And as you wait upon the Lord, you will find strength rising. As you wait upon the Lord, hope will be rekindled that you will see the goodness of the Lord in the land of the living. As you wait upon the Lord, faith will grow that He will turn to you and hear your cry. O Pilgrim, as you wait upon Him, He will come! He will come and He will hold out His hands to you. Listen to His words: "Arise, My darling, My beautiful one, come with Me" (Song of Songs 2:10). Yes, Pilgrim, these words are addressed to you – for He is the One who has redeemed your life from the pit and has crowned you with love and compassion! He is the One who leads you with cords of human kindness, with ties of love. He is like One who lifts a little child to His cheek! And Jesus will take you by the hand, and He will lift you to your feet that you might stand up.

Pilgrim, stand up, for the Spirit has lifted you up! Arise! For those who trust in the name of the Lord our God will rise up and stand firm! For when He lifts you up out of the pit, He sets your feet on a rock and gives you a firm place to stand. For the Word of the Lord is eternal, standing firm in the heavens – and the Word of the Lord is the firm Rock upon which you are standing. Oh, how firm, how solid is this Rock! How this Rock becomes a broad path beneath your feet, where your ankles will be built up, your feeble knees will be strengthened, as He makes your feet like the feet of a deer, and enables you to stand on the heights.

And now that you know the living God, now that you

have beheld His power and glory, you who bring good news to Zion, go up on a high mountain. You who bring good news to Jerusalem, lift up your voice with a shout, lift it up, do not be afraid; and say to the towns of Judah, "Here is your God!" (Isaiah 40:9).

44.
DEAR PILGRIM, DO YOU HEAR THE
SOUND OF WEEPING?

Dear Pilgrim, do you hear the sound of weeping? Do you hear the sound of wailing, of mourning, of grief?

This is the Valley of Baka (Psalm 84:6), a dry valley, a valley without water, the valley of weeping. This is the place where tears flow like a river day and night, where beds are flooded with weeping and couches are drenched with tears, where streams of tears flow from eyes. This is the place where daughters are taught how to wail, where laments are taught to one another. This is the place where ashes are eaten as food and drink is mingled with tears. This is the place where sackcloth is worn and dust is sprinkled on heads. This is the house of mourning, dear Pilgrim.

O Pilgrim, take courage as you pass through this valley. Be heartened, for this is not the sound of worldly sorrow that you hear, this is not the crying of self-pity that leads to death. No Pilgrim, this is a righteous sound. This is godly sorrow.

For streams of tears are flowing from eyes because His law is not obeyed (Psalm 119:136). Mourning over sin in self and mourning over sin in the land, the cry goes up to heaven that all the tears that fall be listed in His scroll and in His record (Psalm 56:8). The hearts of the fathers have been turned away from their children in the land, so here in the Valley of Baka hearts are poured out on the ground in the presence of the Lord, hands are lifted to Him for the lives of their children who are fainting from hunger at every street corner, fainting from a hunger and a thirst for righteousness in the land. For truth has stumbled in the streets, and righteousness stands afar as His laws are disregarded. Is there anyone who can bring comfort? Is there anyone who can build up the wall and stand in the gap?

O Pilgrim, now you are weeping too. Overcome by grief, you are weeping and weeping as you cry out, "Is there no-one?"

Do not weep, dear Pilgrim! See, the Lion of the tribe of Judah, the Root of David, has triumphed! The Righteous One came, full of grace and truth, and after He shouted in victory, "It is finished!", He rose again, He ascended, He has sat down at the right hand of God, and since that time He waits for His enemies to be made a footstool for His feet. And now that God's love has been poured out into our hearts through the Holy Spirit, who has been given to us (Romans 5:5), we overflow with hope by the power of the Holy Spirit (Romans 15:13).

For as we travel through the Valley of Baka, it becomes a place of springs. As we acknowledge the Lord, as we press on to acknowledge Him, as surely as the sun rises He will appear, He will come to us like the winter rains, like the spring rains that water the earth (Hosea 6:3). In the dry and weary land that you are passing through, as you spread out your hands to Him in your thirst, He will come and He will open your eyes to see the springs of water that He has provided. Where there is no water, He will give you the faith to cry out to Him in your thirst, and He will open up for you an En Hakkore – a caller's spring (Judges 15:18-19)! He will turn the desert into pools of water, and the parched land into flowing springs (Psalm 107:35). The burning sand will become a pool, the thirsty ground bubbling springs (Isaiah 35:7).

Be ever watchful though, dear Pilgrim, as you pass the springs – for not all are His - there are some deceptive brooks (Jeremiah 15:18). These are springs without water, without His life-giving water (2 Peter 2:17). These are springs which will fail. For not only do some forsake the spring of living water, but they dig their own broken cisterns which cannot hold water (Jeremiah 2:13). O Pilgrim, watch out for those who will lead you astray, who mouth empty, boastful words and appeal to the lustful desires of the flesh, serving up to you muddied water out of a polluted well. There is no life in them! The only cure for bad water is to take a new bowl filled with salt and throw it into the spring (2 Kings 2:19-22).

Be patient as you travel through, dear Pilgrim, waiting for the autumn rains. See how the farmer waits for the land to yield its valuable crop, patiently waiting for the autumn and spring rains (James 5:7). Be patient, dear Pilgrim, as you go out weeping, carrying seed to sow, as you sow with tears. For you will reap with songs of joy in the fullness of time, you will return with songs of joy, carrying sheaves with you (Psalm 126:5-6)!

And you will go from strength to strength, until that glorious day when you appear before God in Zion (Psalm 84:7), where He will wipe away all the tears from your face, where you will drink without cost from the spring of the water of life (Revelation 21:6), and where your mourning will turn to laughter (Luke 6:21). And when He comes and places a crown of beauty on your head, instead of ashes (Isaiah 61:3), your joy will know no bounds.

45.
DEAR PILGRIM, ARE YOU READY TO RECEIVE A CROWN?

Dear Pilgrim, are you ready to receive a crown? A crown upon your head? Do you realize that a crown awaits you?

Wide-eyed you may be, but this is the truth in His Word! For when we worship the King of Kings and the Lord of Lords, a King who wears many crowns upon His head, a King who loves to give in abundance, a King who delights to share with His own, how can it be any other way?

Fix your eyes on your King, Pilgrim. Your King, who left all the glory of heaven and emptied Himself, making Himself a servant, and was born in the likeness of man. Your King, your Creator, who rested His head in a manger on the night He was born as the shepherds gathered around to worship Him. As a baby He rested His head in the arms of His mother, Mary, whilst she cared for Him. He rested His head in the arms of Simeon on the day He was circumcised, as Simeon proclaimed Him a light for revelation to the Gentiles and the glory of His people, Israel.

When the time came, and to fulfil all righteousness, His head went under the waters of the River Jordan as He was baptised. As He travelled around teaching and healing during His years of ministry, your King had nowhere to lay His head. Even foxes have dens and birds have nests – but your King, your Creator, had nowhere to lay His head.

Just before Passover, as He was reclining at a table in the home of Simon the Leper, His head was anointed with perfume, preparing Him for burial. For your King was soon to suffer. He was crowned by man, but the crown man set upon His head was of cruel, sharp thorns twisted together. A staff to mock His Kingship was used as a weapon to strike Him on the head again and again. As He hung on the cross, His appearance was disfigured beyond that of any human being. Finally He bowed His head and gave up His spirit.

Whilst He was on the cross, the written charge, "Jesus, King of the Jews", was placed above His head. Yes, this Jesus is King of the Jews, He is King of the Gentiles, He is King of the whole world, and of the heavens above – He is King of Kings and Lord of Lords! For just three days later, the cloth that had been wrapped around the head of the King whilst He lay buried, this cloth lay instead in its place in the empty tomb – for He has risen, He has ascended, and He is coming back again!

Come, daughters of Zion, come out and look, look on

your King wearing a crown! A crown of pure gold! But not just one crown – He is wearing many crowns!

Your King – head of every power and authority. Your King – head of the body, the church. And as our Head is anointed with oil, our cup overflows! For He is the Anointed One, the Messiah, the Christ. His head is the one which is anointed with oil, and as we gather around Him, as we find our place in Him, our cup overflows. And as He wears many crowns, He has many crowns to share with us too.

Pilgrim, are you ready to receive a crown? How He has prepared your head. For your whole head was injured. Open sores, untreated, unclean. Burdened, weighed down, in captivity, your sins were higher than your head. Your head was bowed down to the ground, you sprinkled dust on your head. You had no way to heal yourself. Some tried to dress your wound as though it were not serious, telling you, "Peace!" But this was no remedy, your wound continued to fester, for it was incurable, beyond healing.

But He came! The King who suffered, by His wounds you were healed! He came and He bound up your wounds. He came and He restored you to health. He broke the bars of your yoke, and enabled you to walk with your head held high (Leviticus 26:13).

He redeemed your life from the pit, and He crowned you with love and compassion (Psalm 103:4). His love and His compassion – these already crown you, Pilgrim! Be blessed! For blessings crown the head of the righteous (Proverbs 10:6).

And when He appears, Pilgrim, many more crowns will

He bestow upon His people. You will receive the crown of glory that will never fade away (1 Peter 5:4). The Righteous Judge will award to all those who have longed for His appearing the crown of righteousness (2 Timothy 4:8). You who persevere to the end will receive the crown of life that the Lord has promised to those who love Him (James 1:12). Everlasting joy will crown your head (Isaiah 35:10). He will take away all your grief that you have been carrying with you throughout your pilgrimage, and He will bestow on you a crown of beauty, instead of ashes (Isaiah 61:3). For His people will sparkle in His land like jewels in a crown (Zechariah 9:16).

Listen to Him as He says to His Bride, "Your head crowns you like Mount Carmel" (Song of Songs 7:5). The splendour of Carmel! How He delights in His Bride. She will be a crown of splendour in the Lord's hand, a royal diadem in the hand of her God (Isaiah 62:3). And how she will delight in Him and lay her crowns before His throne, saying, "You are worthy, our Lord and God, to receive glory and honour and power, for You created all things, and by Your will they were created and have their being" (Revelation 4:10-11).

46.
DEAR PILGRIM, WHEN HE COMES, WILL HE FIND FAITH ON THE EARTH?

Dear Pilgrim, when the Son of Man comes, will He find faith on the earth (Luke 18:8)?

O Pilgrim, it is a challenging word that He has brought to us. He told us that many will turn away from the faith in times of trouble. For it is true that not everyone has faith.

Yet Pilgrim, we know that faith comes by hearing, and hearing by the word of God (Romans 10:17). And Pilgrim, your ears have been opened by the One who looked up to heaven with a deep sigh and said, "Ephphatha!"(Mark 7:34). You have heard His voice, you have heard the Word of God!

Pilgrim, remember Mount Carmel and be inspired by a man of faith. Elijah had heard and received the word of God, that rain was coming. In faith he announced to Ahab that there was the sound of an abundance of rain (1 Kings 18:41). Three years of drought, three years where neither dew nor rain had fallen in the land, and now an abundance of rain was proclaimed because of the word of the Lord! For this was a man who lived by faith, and not by sight.

Here, on the top of the mountain, the place where God reveals Himself, the man of God bowed down on the ground, with his face between his knees. He prayed to his God, Pilgrim. What does a man of God pray in such a situation? These words come to mind: "Remember Your word to Your servant, for You have given me hope" (Psalm 119:49). Elijah asked his servant to go and look towards the sea, that their eyes might see the word of the Lord come to pass. His servant looked, came back, and said, "There is nothing." There was no sign.

Elijah continued to pray. He continued to trust in the word of the Lord. He continued to trust in the faithfulness of his God. For no word from God will ever fail. Your word, Lord, is eternal; it stands firm in the heavens (Psalm 119:89). A second time he asked his servant to report what he saw – nothing.

Undaunted, the man of faith in such a situation reminds himself that "the word of the Lord is right and true; He is faithful in all He does" (Psalm 33:4). "And the words of the Lord are flawless, like silver purified in a crucible, like gold refined seven times" (Psalm 12:6). A third time Elijah asked his servant what he saw – nothing.

Faithfully, the man of God, who perseveres in prayer at His throne, cries out, "I wait for the Lord, my whole being waits, and in His word I put my hope" (Psalm 130:5). He calls to mind familiar words of Scripture and brings them before the Lord in humble submission: "My word that goes out from My mouth will not return to Me empty, but will accomplish what I desire and achieve the purpose for which I sent it" (Isaiah 55:11). A fourth time there was no response to Elijah's prayers.

Still he did not waver in unbelief regarding the promise of God, but he was strengthened in his faith and gave glory to God, for he was fully persuaded that God had the power to do what He had promised (Romans 4:20-21). He knew that even though heaven and earth may pass away, His words will never pass away (Mark 13:31). A fifth time Elijah was told there was still no sign.

He held unswervingly to his hope, for he knew that He who promised is faithful (Hebrews 10:23). The man of faith in such a situation prays aloud for all to hear, "As for God, His way is perfect: the Lord's word is flawless; He shields all who take refuge in Him" (2 Samuel 22:31). As he prays, he takes up his shield of faith to extinguish the flaming arrows from the evil one, who is whispering, "Did God really say He would send rain?" A sixth time Elijah's servant went to look towards the sea. Nothing.

The man of faith continues knocking, continues seeking, continues asking that the Lord bring to pass the word He has spoken. He knows that God will bring about justice for His chosen ones, who cry out to Him day and night. He knows that the Lord will not keep putting them off, that His God will see that they get justice, and quickly (Luke 18:7-8). A seventh time Elijah's servant went to look towards the sea.

The servant came running back to the man of God,

breathless with excitement. He had seen something. An abundance of rain was the promise. What was it that could be seen? The skies filled with ominous dark clouds? No – a single cloud! A cloud as small as a man's hand was rising from the sea. Do not despise the day of small things, dear Pilgrim. For from this cloud as small as a man's hand, an abundance of rain would fall over the land. Rejoice that the Lord had heard the cry of the man of faith!

Dear Pilgrim, here, atop Mount Carmel, the mountain of faith, the mountain of belief, He tested the faith of the man of God, and perseverance was produced as a result! What a thing of beauty faith in Him is! Is it any wonder that Mount Carmel is known as a mountain of splendour (Isaiah 35:2)? O Pilgrim, may we follow the example of this man of faith, for Elijah was a man, just like us. May we join the Psalmist in this victorious cry: "I waited patiently for the Lord; He turned to me and heard my cry" (Psalm 40:1).

47.
DEAR PILGRIM, DO YOU NEED BUILDING UP?

Dear Pilgrim, do you need building up? Are you discouraged by so much of what you see in the visible church? By those who profess to know Him, and yet neither proclaim Him in truth, nor worship Him in spirit? By those who have a form of godliness, but deny its power?

Surely the need has never been greater for the wailing women to come to mourn and lament over the ruined houses (Jeremiah 9:17-19). Surely the need has never been greater for them to weep and wail over houses that have fallen with a great crash when the rain came down, the streams rose and the winds blew and beat against them, for they were built on sand.

But Pilgrim, take comfort as you look out across the devastation of the landscape - for He is shaking created things, He is shaking the idols from the land, He is shaking the very foundations of the earth. He is doing this so that what cannot be shaken may remain, for we are receiving a Kingdom that cannot be shaken. And precious Pilgrim, do not neglect to take heed of this word of wisdom: "Build yourselves up in your most holy faith!" (Jude 20).

It is only in your most holy faith that the building up can take place. When man builds apart from God, looking to make a name for himself, it leads to judgement (Genesis 11:4). Yet even when David desired to build a house for God, the Lord told him that instead, He would build a house for David, and establish the throne of his kingdom for ever (1 Chronicles 17:10). So the Temple was destroyed and raised again in three days (John 2:19) – and He Himself laid as a foundation in Zion a stone, a tested stone, a precious cornerstone for a sure foundation.

He brought revelation that Jesus Christ is the Son of the Living God to man, and on this Rock He began to build His church. And just as He began to build His church by the revelation of Jesus Christ through faith, so too the church is built up in the same way (Colossians 2:6-7), through the ministry of the Holy Spirit (Ephesians 4:4-16, 1 Corinthians 14:12,26) and the word of His grace (Acts 20:32).

But some have built on the foundations with wood, hay and straw - and the walls are in need of repair. The word of God is like a hammer that breaks a rock into pieces, the word of God will destroy the false idols - land, land, land, hear the word of God! Otherwise, He will breathe on the walls of wood, hay and straw with the fiery breath of His mouth and they will be burnt up.

The walls can be built up again. The Repairer of Broken Walls will rebuild the walls of faith. He will reveal Himself to those who believe He exists and that He rewards those who earnestly seek Him. To those who do not refuse Him who speaks, to those whose hearts and flesh cry out for the living God, to those who come to Him as children asking Him for His good gifts, He will manifest Himself. He will not quench a faintly burning wick. He will breathe upon it and say, "Receive the Holy Spirit", and it will be fanned into flame.

To those who tarry in Jerusalem, acknowledging their lack of power, and their absolute need for His outpouring upon them, He will come! To those who see their emptiness, their brokenness, their need to be filled, to be empowered by Him, to be emboldened by Him, to be directed by Him and instructed by Him, He will come! To those who are not ashamed of their thirst or their hunger for Him, He will come! But we must wait upon Him. We must seek Him. We must ask Him. We must keep knocking at the door. Oh, for a touch from Him! Tarry, dear Pilgrim, tarry in Jerusalem. But come, He will. And the mustard seed of faith will grow and bear beautiful fruit unto Him.

Dear Pilgrim, unless the Lord builds the house, those who build it labour in vain. Indeed, it is the Father Himself who is seeking for those who will worship Him in spirit and in truth, through the Spirit of Truth. So come to Him, dear Pilgrim, come to Him. For Jesus Christ is a living Stone, He is the Master Builder, and we are His house, if we hold on to our courage and the hope of which we boast. Pilgrim, do not lose heart! Do not be discouraged! You who call on the Lord, give Him no rest and give yourselves no rest until the building is complete. Let us offer Him our broken spirits, our broken, contrite hearts. He will not despise this. And may it please Him to build up the walls of Zion.

48.

DEAR PILGRIM, ARE YOU PASSING THROUGH THE GATES?

Dear Pilgrim, are you passing through the gates on your pilgrimage? Are you moving on in your journey with Him? Are you being led by His Spirit?

O Pilgrim, He has brought you through so many different gates, and each gate that you have passed through brings Him great glory. Each gate that you have passed through reveals how He has enabled you to overcome the world. Each gate speaks a testimony of His work. For He is breaking open the way for you, leading the way for you.

Do you remember where you were when He first came and called you? You were at the gates of death (Psalm 9:13), precious Pilgrim, for you were dead in your transgressions. Oh, what dark gates these were. Gates in the depths of the earth. Gates at the roots of the mountains. Gates that were locked and kept you imprisoned.

Ah, but He came. He came, and He called you. And you cried out to Him in your distress...and He came and broke down those gates of bronze, He cut through the bars of iron and He set you free (Psalm 107:16). He lifted you up from those gates of death. Glory!

You were then faced with a choice of two gates – a wide gate, with many people walking through, or a small gate, leading to a narrow path, with few walking along (Matthew 7:13-14). O Pilgrim! What joy that you went through the narrow gate. He Himself is that gate (John 10:9). Oh, glory to the King of Kings - for this road leads to life, and you are walking along it! You entered with thanksgiving – and He has made you righteous, for it is only the righteous who may enter through this gate (Psalm 118:19-20).

He brought you to the city gate, where your Kinsman-Redeemer declared before witnesses that you would be His bride. And the witnesses declared a blessing of fruitfulness upon you (Ruth 4:11). How you love to come to the city gates, for it is here that you have listened to wisdom crying aloud and making her speech (Proverbs 1:20-21). You have listened, and you have kept your heart teachable. And as you have faithfully been walking in the good works that He prepared in advance for you to do, there have been blessed occasions when these works have brought you praise at the city gates (Proverbs 31:31). But these occasions have been few and far between – for just as He suffered outside the city gate to make the people holy through His own blood, so you too have gone outside, bearing the disgrace that He bore, sharing in His sufferings (Hebrews 13:12-13). For the city gates are not your destination.

Pilgrim, there are gates which are blessed beyond all gates, and it is these gates that we are walking towards. For it is true, the Lord does love all the dwellings of Jacob. Yet it is the gates of Zion that He loves more than anywhere else (Psalm 87:2). For it is here that He has installed His King on His holy mountain (Psalm 2:6), at the very heart of God - Yahweh-Shammah (Ezekiel 48:35). The Lord is there!

It is all too easy on our pilgrimage to tarry at other gates on our ascent to Zion – gates where we can become too easily satisfied with what we have, not realising there is a greater freedom awaiting us. Gates where we can find ourselves falling into captivity, gates where the enemy would seek to waylay us that he might rob and steal us of the full inheritance awaiting us. But how He takes care of us! He opens our eyes to our captivity, and then we find ourselves being carried to the gate which is called Beautiful, asking Him for healing...and in the name of Jesus Christ of Nazareth we arise once more and go on our way, walking and leaping and praising God (Acts 3:2-8).

As we journey through many gates, Pilgrim, this is where we must heed the call to lift up our heads (Psalm 24:9). Lift up our heads! Our King will pass through these gates ahead of us. O Pilgrim, pass through, pass through the gates! Build up the highway, remove the stones, raise a banner for the nations (Isaiah 62:10). For it is the gates of Zion that we are heading towards. The gates of

Zion....gates that always stand open, they are never shut, day or night (Isaiah 60:11). These gates of Zion – they have a name - it is "Praise" (Isaiah 60:18)! Pilgrim, there is a day coming when we will stand in the gates of Daughter Zion, and rejoice in His salvation (Psalm 9:14). O, what a day that will be! As we await that day, let our praises to Him never cease, as we shout our grateful praise to Him, and say, "Salvation comes from the Lord!"

49.
DEAR PILGRIM, DO YOU HAVE OIL IN YOUR LAMP?

Dear Pilgrim, do you have oil in your lamp? Have you remembered to take not only your lamp, but oil in jars with you, as you await the arrival of the Bridegroom? Do you have oil to keep your lamp from going out?

O Pilgrim, let us heed His words of warning. When He returns, may we be like the wise virgins - they had oil in their lamps when the Bridegroom returned at midnight. They went in with Him to the wedding banquet. May we not be like the foolish virgins - they were on their way to buy oil for their lamps when the doors were shut. May we be keeping watch on the oil in our lamps.

There is only one place to go for the oil in our lamps – to Him! For He promises He will send the olive oil, enough to satisfy fully (Joel 2:19), so let the wise store up the olive oil (Proverbs 21:20). Let us come to Him and ask Him to satisfy us fully with His oil. And as our lamps burn with His oil, we will begin to wonder how we ever lived without it.

For the oil of the Holy Spirit reveals that He is present. It was Jacob who poured oil upon the stone at Bethel as he exclaimed, "How awesome is this place! This is none other than the house of God; this is the gate of heaven" (Genesis 28:17-18). O Pilgrim, let us ever be in wonder and awe that He would send His Spirit to dwell inside of us, that He might be present in us!

The oil of the Holy Spirit makes faces shine (Psalm 104:15). When He pours out His oil on His people, their faces shine from His presence. The face of Moses was radiant because he had spoken with the Lord (Exodus 34:29), but he would veil his face for the glory would pass away. But we, who with unveiled faces contemplate the Lord's glory, are being transformed into His image with ever-increasing glory, which comes from the Lord, who is the Spirit (2 Corinthians 3:18). Oh, let us ask that He would make His face shine upon us that His glory may be reflected on our faces!

The oil of the Holy Spirit soothes our wounds (Isaiah 1:6). The Samaritan poured oil upon the wounds of the man, who was attacked by robbers, as he travelled from Jerusalem to Jericho (Luke 10:34). It is by His wounds that we have been healed (1 Peter 2:24), as He pours out His Holy Spirit upon us. Let us come and ask for the soothing touch of His Holy Spirit upon our wounds, the healing balm of Gilead.

The oil of the Holy Spirit brings cleansing. When a diseased person was brought before the priest for cleansing, oil was placed on their right ear lobe, their right thumb, their right toe and on their head in order for them to be pronounced clean (Leviticus 14:15-18). O Pilgrim, as He pours His Holy Spirit upon you, be cleansed!

The oil of the Holy Spirit keeps the light of the lamps burning (Exodus 27:20). Clear oil of pressed olives was used for the light so that the lamps in the tabernacle were kept burning continually (Leviticus 24:2). A lamp is set on its stand and gives light to everyone in the house. As He pours out His Holy Spirit upon us, our light shines before others that they may see our good deeds and glorify our Father in heaven (Matthew 5:15-16). May our lamps shine brightly before others, dear Pilgrim!

The oil of the Holy Spirit brings a boldness to His people (Acts 4:31). As He pours out His Holy Spirit upon us, so we will be given the confidence in Him to speak the word of God boldly to others. Pilgrim, let us ask Him to make us as bold as lions through the power of His Spirit (Proverbs 28:1)!

The oil of the Holy Spirit brings joy to His people. For as He has been anointed with the oil of joy (Hebrews 1:9), so too as He pours out His Spirit upon His people, He bestows on them the oil of joy, instead of mourning (Isaiah 61:3). O Pilgrim, let us come and shout for joy on the heights of Zion; let us rejoice in the bounty of the Lord – the olive oil that He has provided (Jeremiah 31:12)!

For our God provides for the poor from His bounty (Psalm 68:10). He promises that His people will be filled with His bounty (Jeremiah 31:14). So as we await the return of the Bridegroom, let us keep looking to Him, asking that He will open the heavens, the storehouse of His bounty. And let us live by the Spirit, keeping in step with the Spirit, not grieving the Holy Spirit, not quenching the Spirit, but being filled with the Spirit. Then when the Bridegroom returns, we will be invited in to share in the wedding banquet!

50.
DEAR PILGRIM, ARE YOU KEEPING IN STEP WITH THE SPIRIT?

Dear Pilgrim, are you keeping in step with the Spirit? Or are you running ahead up the mountain? Are you ever mindful of your need for Him and dependence upon Him, or have you returned to the folly of trusting in your own strength?

O Pilgrim, it is glorious to be atop the mountain peaks where He reveals Himself to His children. To feast your eyes upon magnificent panoramic views, to feel the breeze on your face, to taste the fresh air in your mouth – there is nothing more exhilarating. But take care, precious Pilgrim, that you ascend in step with Him, in response to His call. It may yet be His desire for you to dwell in the valleys awhile. Do not despise the valleys, O Pilgrim. He goes down to look at the new growth in the valley to see if the vines have budded or the pomegranates are in bloom (Song of Songs 6:11). The valleys are a place of growth!

Pilgrim, heed the warning – do not allow the pride of

your heart to deceive you, that you make your home on the heights (Obadiah 1:3). Unless the Lord builds the house, the builders labour in vain. Do not yield to the temptation to trust in your own strength, your own flesh. Take heed, Pilgrim, for there is another who makes use of the mountain summits - the enemy of our souls.

It was he who, through Balak, called Balaam to the rocky peaks that the people of Israel might be cursed. Balaam, a sorcerer and diviner, was called up to Bamoth Baal, the heights of Baal, from where he could see part of the people of God (Numbers 22:41). They were camped in the Valley of Shittim below, along the east side of the Jordan across from Jericho in the plains of Moab. O Pilgrim, what a foolish endeavour this was, to attempt to curse those whom the Lord had blessed! For the Lord would not listen to this sorcerer and practiser of divination who loved the wages of wickedness. Instead, the Lord caused Balaam to bless the people of Israel.

Balaam was called up the mountain by the enemy of our souls a second time, this time to the field of Zophim on the top of the Pisgah mountain range. A second time the Lord ensured that Balaam blessed the people of Israel. God is not a man, that He should lie, nor a son of man, that He should change His mind. He had blessed His people, and no mere man could change that.

Balaam responded to a third call up the mountains from the enemy of our souls, to Peor, another Moabite mountain. This time, Balaam did not resort to sorcery but turned his face towards the desert and looked out. When he saw Israel encamped tribe by tribe, he saw the tabernacle of the Lord at their centre, the dwelling-place of God amongst His people. Israel, encamped in the Valley of Shittim, had the presence of God with them! As the eyes of Balaam took in this glorious sight, the Spirit of God came upon him and he uttered words of profound depth and revelation – expressing the truth that this people of God encamped in the Valley below were blessed in abundance, as had been true of the first people of God on the mountain in Eden – for the Lord their God was with them.

"How beautiful are your tents, O Jacob,
your dwelling-places, O Israel!

Like valleys they spread out,
Like gardens beside a river,
Like aloes planted by the Lord,
Like cedars beside the waters.
Water will flow from their buckets;
Their seed will have abundant water"
(Numbers 24:5-7)

There are many occasions when the Lord calls His people to dwell in the valleys that His purposes might be fulfilled through them. Those on the mountain were working against the purposes of God, yet in His Sovereignty the Lord caused them to bless His people in abundance. The Lord foils the plans of the nations and thwarts the purposes of the people (Psalm 33:10), because it is the Lord's purpose that prevails (Proverbs 19:21).

It was on this same mountain range not long

afterwards that the Lord Himself called His own servant to come up. Moses, whom the Lord knew face to face, ascended Mount Nebo in response to the call of the Lord, in step with His Spirit (Deuteronomy 34:1). And when Moses was atop the mountain peak, having climbed it in the strength of the Lord alone, the Lord Himself came and showed Moses the whole land of Promise – a land of mountains and valleys that drinks rain from heaven (Deuteronomy 11:11). For precious Pilgrim, the truth is that when we dwell in the valleys, having had revelation from the peaks, we can see more clearly that He tabernacles with us – and He fills us with joy in His presence whether we are on the mountains above or in the valleys below. For the valleys drink rain from heaven, just as the mountains do.

So Pilgrim, remember that those who are led by the Spirit are the children of God. Allow Him to lead you – whether it be to the mountains or the valleys, to the deserts or to the fertile fields. For blessed are those who have learned to acclaim Him, who walk in the light of His presence (Psalm 89:15).

51.
DEAR PILGRIM, DO YOU TREMBLE AT THE SHAKING?

Dear Pilgrim, do you tremble at the shaking? The shaking you currently see, the shaking that will come? Come, as we walk this dusty pilgrim road together, let us contemplate the mountains.

Ancient, from old. How they rise from the plains, imperious, towering, majestic. Silent, brooding, not speaking of all they have seen over the years. Who can know their thoughts? Solid and unyielding, their presence inspires awe as we make our way along this path. They remind us of our fleeting presence here on earth, of our insignificance, our smallness. They point us to the greatness of Him – for He created them by the power of His Word. The mountain peaks belong to Him (Psalm 95:4), all of them. They depend on Him for their existence – for He sustains all things by His powerful Word – all things. They eagerly drink from His hand – for it is He who waters them from His upper chambers

(Psalm 104:13). They even sing for joy before Him (Psalm 98:8), as He comes to judge the earth.

But take note, Pilgrim. As He looks at the earth, just looks at it, it trembles, and as He reaches out His hand and touches the mountains – they smoke (Psalm 104:32) before Him. As He comes in judgment, can it be? The mountains – they are melting like wax (Psalm 97:5) before Him! The earth – it gives way, and the mountains – they are falling into the heart of the sea (Psalm 46:2-3)! The mountains are quaking – quaking in fear, Pilgrim – quaking, as the waters of the sea roar and foam and surge. O Pilgrim! Even the mountains are as nothing before Him, His might, His justice, His holiness! It is no wonder, Pilgrim, that as He comes in judgment, the wicked will cry out to the mountains and the rocks, "Fall on us and hide us from the face of Him who sits on the throne and from the wrath of the Lamb! For the great day of their wrath has come, and who can withstand it?" (Revelation 6:16-17).

But God has a mountain of His own. Just as He is making distinctions amongst the people, He is making distinctions amongst the mountains. And on this particular mountain, His holy mountain, He has installed His King (Psalm 2:6)! He will establish this mountain as the highest of the mountains, and it will be exalted above the hills (Isaiah 2:2).

Yet this mountain is called an outcast (Jeremiah 30:17). No one cares for her. She is avoided and shunned, scorned and derided by those around her. She has become an object of contempt. The taunts of all nations fall upon her, as she is despised and mocked by her enemies. Hear the word of the Lord, you mountains, you people! This is the mountain over which the Lord burns with jealousy (Zechariah 8:2-3), and He will return and dwell in her.

It is no wonder that Mount Bashan, that majestic, rugged mountain, is gazing in envy (Psalm 68:15-16) at the mountain where God chooses to reign, where the Lord Himself will dwell forever. For the Lord loves this mountain more than all the other dwellings of Jacob (Psalm 87:2). It is on this mountain that the Lord bestows His blessing and life forevermore (Psalm 133:3). It is on this mountain that there will be deliverance (Joel 2:32).

Mount Zion.

But who may ascend this mountain of the Lord (Psalm 24:3)? O Pilgrim, we have confidence that we can, for we are trusting in His King, and He has cleansed our hands and He has purified our hearts (Psalm 24:4)! And as we continue to trust in Him, Pilgrim, He makes us like Mount Zion which cannot be shaken but endures forever (Psalm 125:1)! Other mountains will be shaken and fall – but Mount Zion will remain! We, too, like Mount Zion, may walk this pilgrim path as outcasts. Those with no understanding will envy that His Spirit dwells in us, that as King He reigns over us - yet rejoice, Pilgrim! Rejoice, for how great is the love the Father has lavished on us that we should be called children of God! And Pilgrim, oh, even your name points to this! For those whose hearts are set on pilgrimage, whose strength is in Him, are blessed (Psalm 84:5,7) – they will go from strength to strength till each appears before Him in Zion!

Pilgrim, fear not at the shaking. It is necessary, so that what cannot be shaken may remain. And so the redeemed of the Lord shall walk in Zion (Isaiah 35:9-10), those the Lord has rescued will return. They will enter Zion with singing, everlasting joy will crown their heads. Gladness and joy will overtake them, and sorrow and sighing will flee away!

> *Indeed, of Zion it will be said,*
> *"This one and that one were born in her,*
> *and the Most High Himself will establish her."*
> *The Lord will write in the register of the peoples:*
> *"This one was born in Zion."*
> *(Psalm 87:5-6)*

52.
DEAR PILGRIM, HAVE YOU BEEN WITH HIM?

Dear Pilgrim, have you been with Him? Have you sought Him out to spend time alone with Him, just as the Son sought out His Father through the Spirit that He might hear from Him? Ah, Pilgrim, I can see that you have!

For just as the dew drenches the grass as a sign that He has walked amongst His creation in the early morning, calling the sun to burst forth and chase away the shadows of darkness, so too the dew of Hermon covers you – for you have been on Mount Zion. Though the climb was difficult, you lingered on the summit, dear Pilgrim. You waited upon Him. You yearned for His presence. And ever faithful to His promise, He came, for He delights to reveal Himself to those who hunger and thirst after Him. In joy you fed on the living Bread – and heavenly dew settled on you as you faithfully collected your daily manna. His Word descended like dew upon you, a sign of

His favour towards you (Proverbs 19:12). Strengthened in Him, sustained by Him, comforted through Him, you were filled with Him as you drank thirstily and deeply from Him.

O Pilgrim, you may have descended from the mountain top down to the valley here below, but that is because so many people live in the valleys. And the remnant of Jacob will be in the midst of many peoples like dew from the Lord, like showers on the grass, which do not wait for anyone or depend on man (Micah 5:7). For you wait upon Him alone, your dependence is on Him alone as you seek to serve Him alone.

And so you walk in the midst of many peoples, no longer your own but His, for He bought you at a price. He leads you as a captive in Christ's triumphal procession. O Pilgrim, never forget, this is a triumphal procession! He is leading the way, striding forth in victory, for He is our Forerunner, our Pioneer! You may not hear the heavenly trumpets down here in the valleys, but they are resounding loudly and clearly around the throne of God and of the Lamb! You may not see the crowds lining the streets waving and cheering as this triumphal procession passes through, but rest assured, dear Pilgrim, a great multitude will stand before the throne and before the Lamb, wearing white robes, holding palm branches in their hands, and shouting out in a loud voice, "Salvation belongs to our God, who sits on the throne, and to the Lamb!"

A triumphal procession....yet this procession brings with it an aroma of death to those who are perishing.

Death! O Pilgrim, those who love the darkness because their deeds are evil will recoil as the aroma of this triumphal procession wafts around them, they will hate this fragrance for fear that their deeds will be exposed. This is not a procession that will receive the acclaim of the world. For the world hated Him first, and as you follow your Pioneer, chosen out of the world by Him, no longer belonging to the world, it will hate you too. What fellowship can light have with darkness?

But the fellowship of the Father, the Son and the Holy Spirit is yours, and as Christ's triumphal procession brings you into the presence of other pilgrims, a life-giving fragrance will perfume the air. Amongst the many who have received Him and believed in His Name, you will encounter the few who have been with Him, and your spirit will awaken as you recognise Him in them. You will catch glimpses of Him through their eyes – from those whose eyes forever show the marks of having seen Him, who have beheld His power and His glory. Your heart will leap as you see how He has inscribed their hands – those whose hands have touched His wounds, the wounds in His hands and His side. You will be encouraged, comforted and exhorted as you hear His voice at times speak through their words – from those who have heard His voice speaking to them and did not harden their hearts.

Yet as much as this is true of them, dear Pilgrim, it is also true of you. There is no hiding the truth that you have been with Him. For when you speak, your accent gives you away (Matthew 26:73). You speak to testify about Him, for this is what He calls those who have been with Him to do (John 15:27). Your speech has a cadence which has been carved out by Him, and there is no mistaking the heavenly lilt to each word, for it is an accent rich with a timbre of wisdom. Dear Pilgrim, it is a joy to listen to your speech as each word lifts the heart and eyes of other pilgrims heavenwards.

O Pilgrim, as He leads you captive in His triumphal procession, you are with Him where He is (John 17:24), following Him wherever He leads, not running ahead of Him, for you are led by His Spirit.

Pilgrim, as you have been with Him and you are with Him, so too you will be with Him – for He is coming back, and He will take you to be with Him that you also may be where He is (John 14:3). May He strengthen your heart so that you will be blameless and holy in the presence of our God and Father when the Lord Jesus comes with all His holy ones.

53.
DEAR PILGRIM, HAVE YOU NOTICED THE BEAUTY OF YOUR FEET?

Dear Pilgrim, have you noticed the beauty of your feet? They may be hot and dusty, for you have walked a long way, but do you see how beautiful they are?

Ah, the quizzical look in your eye...what are you wearing on your feet, Pilgrim? You have not been walking barefoot all these many miles, otherwise your feet would be scratched and torn. Your feet have not been dressed in ordinary shoes, for we worship no ordinary God. Pilgrim, you are wearing sandals!

Remember, Pilgrim, when He first called you, when you realized you were standing on Holy ground, He told you to take off your sandals. How awesome was that moment when He revealed His Holiness to you, when you clearly saw for the first time your own uncleanness before Him. Remember how with trembling fingers you unstrapped your sandals as you bowed low before Him. Our God is Holy, Holy, Holy, and we cannot bring

211

anything with us before Him that is soiled and dirty. So those sandals which had been walking in the ways of darkness and wickedness had to be removed. They had to be taken off. They had to be discarded.

O Pilgrim, do you then remember how He came to you and He Himself put sandals of fine leather on you (Ezekiel 16:10)? These were no ordinary sandals that He came to you with. They were of the finest leather, for He provides only the best. Sandals of the finest leather, providing great comfort to your feet, moulding themselves to your feet.

Yet it was not just their quality that was significant. For the sandals that He gave you demonstrated that you were no longer a slave, a slave to sin, for slaves were given nothing to wear upon their feet. The sandals that He gave you announced before those watching that now you were a son – a son adopted into His family, given the prestige of wearing sandals upon your feet (Luke 15:22)! O Pilgrim, we are not worthy to stoop down and untie the straps of His sandals (Mark 1:7), yet He came and knelt down at our feet as He dressed them in sandals of sonship, and declared in great joy, "How beautiful your sandalled feet!" (Song of Songs 7:1). What love is this?

Wearing these sandals of sonship, your feet have been released from snares (Psalm 25:15), and instead you have been walking about in freedom because you have sought out His precepts (Psalm 119:45). The path has become broad beneath you so that your ankles have not given way (Psalm 18:36). Your feet have been set in a spacious place (Psalm 31:8) as you have followed the lamp of His Word giving light to your path (Psalm 119:105). Your feet, fitted with the readiness that comes from the gospel of peace (Ephesians 6:15), have been walking in the good works that He prepared in advance for you to do (Ephesians 2:10). On occasion it has been necessary for you to shake the dust off your feet (Matthew 10:14) but have you noticed, dear Pilgrim, never once have you needed new sandals? For He has been sustaining you every step of the way (Deuteronomy 29:5), as you walk in your sandals of the finest leather, sandals of sonship.

Pilgrim, there is a further meaning behind His giving you sandals to wear. For unlike the idols which have feet, but cannot walk (Psalm 115:7), our God has been walking ever since He created the world. He walked with Adam and Eve in the Garden in the cool of the day (Genesis 3:8). He promised His people, "I will walk among you and be your God and you will be My people" (Leviticus 26:12). He walked amongst the lost sheep of Israel calling out those who would hear His voice. He walked on the water, terrifying His disciples, revealing His divinity. He walked to Golgotha to bear the penalty for our sin. His pierced feet walked with the disciples to Emmaus. Today He walks amongst His churches (Revelation 2:1), speaking words of encouragement, rebuke and exhortation to those who have ears to hear what the Spirit is saying to the churches.

Just as He walks, then, dear Pilgrim, we too must walk and follow our Good Shepherd, as He leads the way for us, outside the city gate, to bear the disgrace He bore (Hebrews 13:13). Let us ask Him where He is walking, and let us follow. And do not fail to notice, dear Pilgrim, that as He walks He leads us upwards, ever heading towards Zion.

For the day is coming when His feet will once again stand on the Mount of Olives (Zechariah 14:4), when He will gather us to be with Him, and when we will declare, "Our feet are standing in your gates, Jerusalem!" (Psalm 122:2). For this is the place of His throne and the place for the soles of His feet, the place where He will dwell among His people for ever (Ezekiel 43:7).

54.
DEAR PILGRIM, ARE YOU APPROACHING THE VALLEY OF DEEP DARKNESS?

Dear Pilgrim, are you approaching the valley of deep darkness? Does your heart lurch within you as you are confronted with this valley? As your enemy pursues you, crushing you to the ground, forcing you towards the valley of darkness, do your fears rise? As the gates of this valley of deepest darkness open for you as you pass through, does your courage fade?

Pilgrim, there is no need to fear any evil as you walk through this valley, for He is with you, His rod and His staff will comfort you. Listen to His Word of comfort: "Never will I leave you, never will I forsake you".

As you walk through this valley, Pilgrim, are any memories being stirred in your mind? Does any of this look familiar to you? In this valley of darkness, there are those who rebel against the light, who do not know its ways or stay on its paths (Job 24:13). All their days they eat in darkness, with great frustration, affliction and anger (Ecclesiastes 5:17). They are prisoners, sitting in darkness, suffering in iron chains (Psalm 107:10).

Ah, Pilgrim, I see a look of realization dawning upon you – this is where you and I used to dwell! We were willing subjects of the dominion of darkness. We did not want to come to the light, for fear that our deeds of evil would be exposed (John 3:19-20). We thought the darkness would hide us. We thought even light would become night around us, and that we could keep our faces concealed. We committed our deeds of sin in the dark, and made friends with the terrors of darkness (Job 24:13-17).

And then we saw something, dear Pilgrim. The people walking in darkness have seen a great light; on those living in the land of deep darkness a light has dawned (Isaiah 9:2). And then we heard something, dear Pilgrim. We heard Him call! He called us! He called us out of darkness into His wonderful light (1 Peter 2:9)! And as we turned our faces towards the Light, He brought us out of darkness, out of utter darkness, and broke away our chains (Psalm 107:14)!

Pilgrim, take heart from the fact that your dislike of this valley is so intense. This is a sign of His grace towards you! For He has rescued you from the dominion of darkness and brought you into the kingdom of the Son He loves (Colossians 1:13)! You are now a child of the light and a child of the day. You do not belong to the night or to the darkness (1 Thessalonians 5:5)!

For the Lord our God is making distinctions, Pilgrim.

He is making distinctions between the righteous and the wicked, between those who serve God and those who do not (Malachi 3:18). At the dawn of creation, He saw that the light was good and He separated the light from the darkness (Genesis 1:4). He brought a plague of darkness upon Egypt, a darkness that could be felt, so that the people of Egypt could not see anyone else or move about for three days. Yet all the Israelites had light in the places where they lived (Exodus 10:21-23). As He delivered His people from Egypt and brought them to the sea, His pillar of cloud stood between the armies of Egypt and Israel. Throughout the night the cloud brought darkness to the one side and light to the other (Exodus 14:19-20). See, darkness covers the earth and thick darkness is over the peoples, but the Lord rises upon you and His glory appears over you (Isaiah 60:2). The Lord our God is making distinctions, Pilgrim.

So do not fear as you pass through the valley of deep darkness, dear Pilgrim. This is no longer the place of your abode. You are now a foreigner, an alien, a stranger, to this valley. It no longer has any hold over you. For the darkness is passing, the true Light is already shining (1 John 2:8). For He who is the Light of the world is with you, and His words are true: "Whoever follows Me will never walk in darkness, but will have the light of life" (John 8:12). So even here, as you cross the valley of deep darkness, the Light of Life is with you, precious Pilgrim. The Light shines in the darkness, and the darkness has not overcome it (John 1:5)! He is your lamp, and He will turn your darkness into light (2 Samuel 22:29). Even in

217

darkness, light dawns for the upright, for those who are gracious and compassionate and righteous (Psalm 112:4).

So take courage, dear Pilgrim. You will pass through this valley. For this is not your home. You are heading for the Holy City, the new Jerusalem, whose gates are never shut, for there will be no night there (Revelation 21:25). No night! For God is light, and in Him there is no darkness at all (1 John 1:5). There will be no night there, and there will be no need for a lamp, or the sun, for He Himself will give the light (Revelation 22:5)! What a glorious hope this is to meditate upon as you pass through this valley.

55.
DEAR PILGRIM, ARE YOU JOURNEYING WITH EL BETHEL?

Dear Pilgrim, are you journeying with El Bethel? Is the God of the House of God the One who leads you? Is He leading you safely Home to your Father's household?

O Pilgrim, let us recall the blessed place of Bethel. Jacob had run away from his brother, Esau, who wanted to kill him. As the sun set, Jacob stopped for the night at Bethel. Let us remind ourselves of the countless stars in the night sky speaking of the promise of numerous descendants for Abraham, as Jacob, the grandson of the promise, settled down to sleep (Genesis 28:11).

Pilgrim, you are familiar with the dream that Jacob had as he slept here, of the stairway resting on the earth, its top reaching to heaven, and the angels of God ascending and descending on it. You remember the promise the Lord gave to Jacob as He stood above the stairway, confirming the promise given to Abraham – that He would give him the land upon which he was lying, descendants as numerous as the dust of the earth, that all nations would be blessed through him and his offspring, and that God Himself would be with him to accomplish all He had promised (Genesis 28:13-15).

As Jacob awakened from his dream, he said, "How awesome is this place! This is none other than the house of God; this is the gate of heaven!" (Genesis 28:17). O Pilgrim, these words spoken by Jacob demonstrate the revelation he had been given. He spoke, not in words taught by human wisdom, but in words taught by the Spirit, interpreting the spiritual truth that had been given to Him. For Jesus declared of Himself, "I am the gate" (John 10:9). He said, "Very truly I tell you, you will see heaven open, and the angels of God ascending and descending on the Son of Man" (John 1:51). He is the Way, the Truth and the Life, no-one comes to the Father except through Him. It is through Him that the gulf that has existed between man and God since the fall of Adam has been removed. It is through Him that we can be reconciled and come home to our Father!

Jacob took the stone that he had rested his head upon, and he set it up as a pillar. He had rested on the stone. He was weary and burdened, so he had rested his head on the stone. The stone that causes people to stumble and a rock that makes them fall. Yet those who rely on this stone will never be stricken with panic (Isaiah 28:16).

Jacob set this stone up as a pillar. A pillar, to be a witness. For the stones will cry out, "Blessed is He who comes in the Name of the Lord!" (Luke 19:40). Then Jacob poured oil on top of the stone. He anointed it with oil. The oil of the Holy Spirit. Is Jacob not pointing us here to the anointing of the Holy Spirit that would be upon the Stone which the builders rejected but which has become the cornerstone (Acts 10:38)? The anointing to proclaim good news to the poor! The anointing to bind up the broken-hearted, to proclaim freedom for the captives and release from darkness for prisoners, to proclaim the year of the Lord's favour!

Listen, Pilgrim, to the words of Jacob's proclamation: "This stone that I have set up as a pillar will be God's house" (Genesis 28:22). Take note as he calls this place Bethel – the house of God (Genesis 28:19).

For the Son was sent from the Father, filled with the Spirit, to call His people home. Home, a place of belonging, with the Holy God of all creation. Home, a place of beauty, rest, justice and righteousness. Home, where His people are accepted and part of the family, loving and being loved. O Pilgrim, what a home! Yet through Adam this home was forsaken and ever since, we have been restless wanderers on the earth, adrift and homeless, sensing what has been lost because He has set eternity in the hearts of men. What a wretched existence!

But God sent His Son to build a house for His Name (2 Samuel 7:13)! And now, by His great love, we can come into His house, in reverence bowing down before Him! O, how lovely is Your dwelling-place, Lord Almighty! Home, where we are fellow citizens with God's people and members of His household, built on the foundations of the apostles and prophets, with Christ Himself as the chief cornerstone! Home, where we are reconciled with the Father and enjoy His embrace! Clothed with a robe of righteousness, sandals of sonship and a ring of authority! Seated at His banqueting table, for His people feast in the abundance of His house! Home, where those who love Him and obey His teaching enjoy the fellowship of the Father and the Son through the Holy Spirit.

El Bethel, the God of the House of God, has come to us and made His home with us! Can it really be true? O Pilgrim, yes, yes it is true, for He has done it! O Pilgrim, let me say it again, for this is the very heart of the gospel – El Bethel, the God of the House of God, has come to us and made His home with us! Meditate on this, feed on it, drink it in! Will He not also be with us and watch over us on our journey, giving us food to eat and clothes to wear so that we return safely to our Father's household? Surely His goodness and love will follow us all the days of our lives, and we will dwell in the house of the Lord for ever!

> *"As God has said:*
> *'I will live with them*
> *and walk among them,*
> *and I will be their God,*
> *and they will be My people'"*
> *(2 Corinthians 6:16)*

56.
DEAR PILGRIM, ARE YOU WAITING FOR THE BLESSED HOPE?

Dear Pilgrim, are you waiting for the blessed hope? The appearing of the glory of our great God and Saviour, Jesus Christ? Is this your eager desire and hope?

Are you groaning as you wait eagerly? The whole of creation is groaning! It has been groaning right up to the present time. It groans under the weight of the curse upon it, groaning over the decay and death that came into the world through the sin of one man, Adam. It groans every time a thistle grows up and chokes the plants, causing their beauty to be quenched. It groans every time an animal turns killer and feeds on its prey. It groans as it awaits its hope that it will be redeemed from the curse and be brought into the freedom that we ourselves have been brought into.

And we ourselves are groaning. We have the seal of the Spirit upon us, a deposit guaranteeing our future inheritance, we have been brought into the blessed freedom of Christ, but as yet we remain in these mortal bodies. Bodies which are subject to decay and death, for they too remain under the curse. Pilgrim, how we long to be clothed with our heavenly dwelling! How we long for what is mortal to be swallowed up by what is immortal! How we long to be free from these bodies of death! How we long to finally be set free forever from the sinful nature and the daily battle against the flesh. Oh, the yearning to be set free from this body of death, this body which is perishable, this body of dishonour, of weakness! Oh, the hope that awaits us of the resurrected body of life, which will be imperishable, raised in glory, raised in power!

But as we continue to hope for what we do not yet have, let us wait for it patiently (Romans 8:25). Let us heed the call to be patient as we await the Lord's coming. Let us be patient and stand firm, for His coming is near! Let us run with perseverance the race marked out for us, fixing our eyes on Jesus, the author and perfecter of our faith. Let us glory in our sufferings, because we know that suffering produces perseverance. Let us consider it pure joy whenever we face trials of many kinds, because we know that the testing of our faith produces perseverance. May perseverance finish its work so that we may be mature and complete, not lacking anything (James 1:2-4). For His saints who fear Him lack nothing (Psalm 34:9)! Nothing! Oh, how gracious are the mercies of our Lord, that He wants us to be complete in His sight! Let us put to death any grumbling over trials. O Lord, save us from a grumbling spirit.

Let us persevere, so that when we have done the Lord's will, we will receive what He has promised, that we may be confident and unashamed before Him at His coming (1 John 2:28). For if we continue in our faith, established and firm, and do not move from the hope held out in the gospel, we will be presented to Him holy in His sight, without blemish and free from accusation (Colossians 1:22-23). And as we continue in the faith, continuing to look to Him, to trust in Him, He will keep our whole spirit, soul and body blameless at the coming of our Lord Jesus Christ. For the One who calls us is faithful and He will do it (1 Thessalonians 5:23-24)! Blameless, dear Pilgrim! Without blemish! Free from accusation! Unashamed! Confident before Him! O Pilgrim, how can this be possible? Only through Christ, dear Pilgrim, only through Christ. The riches, oh, the glorious riches of this gospel! Oh, what a rich welcome awaits us!

So let us wait eagerly for His coming. Lift up your heads, for your redemption draws near! Times of darkness draw near. Times of great distress draw near. We will be hated by all nations because of Him. Many will turn away from the faith and will betray and hate each other. The love of most will grow cold. But he who stands firm to the end will be saved. Even in a time of great distress, it will be possible to stand firm, for the Rock beneath your feet is ever firm, it does not change, it does not shake.

Stand firm then, dear Pilgrim, and you will be victorious. For there are the richest of blessings awaiting the one who is victorious. The right to eat from the tree of life. No fear of the second death. Hidden manna. A white stone with a new name written on it. Authority over the nations. Dressed in white. Never blotted out from the book of life. Acknowledged before the Father and His angels by the Son. Made a pillar in the temple of God, never to leave it again. The name of God, the name of the city of God, and the name of the Son's new name written on them. The right to sit with Him on His throne (Revelation 2-3).

Wonderful rich blessings, Pilgrim, who can plumb the depths of the riches of this glorious gospel? Yet in truth...the only desire we have, the reason we wait so eagerly for the blessed hope, for the appearing of the glory of our great God and Saviour, Jesus Christ, is that we will finally see Him face to face. Oh! When all pilgrims have their deepest yearning fulfilled....what a gathering that will be! Yes, there will be trumpets. Yes, there will be shouts of angels. Yes, we will be changed in a flash. But surely all that will be our focus will be Him, His face, His eyes like blazing fire! "My heart says of You, 'Seek His face!' Your face, Lord, I will seek!" (Psalm 27:8).

9 780099 92040